# Contents

0749412895

First published in 1996

Kogan Page Limited
120 Pentonville Road
London N1 9JN

© Janet Gibson, 1996

**British Library Cataloguing in Publication Data**
A CIP record for this book is available from the British Library.
ISBN 0 7494 1289 5

Typeset by Saxon Graphics Ltd, Derby
Printed and bound in Great Britain by Biddles Ltd, Guildford and King's Lynn

# Preface and Acknowledgements

When choosing a course of study it is important to find out all the options open so that you can make an informed decision about the best course of study for you. The method of learning and teaching is just as important as course content. Vocational qualifications are a more practical approach to study than their academic counterparts, and many students prefer this method of learning.

I have therefore written this book to help all those interested in the new general vocational courses and to try to demystify the qualification referred to as GNVQs. The intention is to provide an up-to-date 'one-stop' guide to GNVQs – and how to make a success of them.

There have been many changes to GNVQs during the last two years. I have included all those changes so that the course information contained in this book is up-to-date with the current course offer. I am grateful to NCVQ and SCOTVEC for their help in compiling the information.

Whether you are a student, prospective student, parent or guardian, or in another capacity helping a student to decide on the best course of study, this book will explain:

- the framework and organization of GNVQs
- the latest information on the courses available and the mandatory units for those courses
- the role/requirements of the student
- how GNVQs fit in with progression to work/HE and further qualifications
- the alternatives to GNVQs

I have also included a chapter with tips on how to be a successful student.

Students who have completed GNVQs have remarkable success stories to tell, and I have included a selection of these as a final and fitting chapter to their achievements.

My acknowledgement and thanks for their time go to the following:

My daughter Lucy and my son Sam for reading the manuscript and giving me their invaluable opinion. Also to my daughter for the illustrations in the book.

To my colleagues Nick Steward, Mike Gallagher, Bernice Gummer and Richard Dalton, Tower Hamlets College, London.

Rob Coward, Rachel Thomas, John Hammond and Rachel Hersh at NCVQ, wih particular thanks to Rob Coward and Rachel Thomas for their courteous attention and generous time in answering my questions and helping me ensure accuracy. Phil Cleaver, Alex Poole and Hilary Wight at BTEC. Mike Capel and Kath Mills at C&G. John Dunn and Anita Karadia at RSA. Iain Grant, Stephanie Wilson and Mary MacArthur at SCOTVEC for their courteous attention and generous time in answering my questions and helping me to ensure accuracy. Judith Compton and Lucy Tucker of the GATE Project. Pam Gee, Network SouthCentral. Ann Davey and Ian Rideout, John Ruskin College, Croydon. Russ Ellis, Deyes High School, Maghull, Liverpool. Graham Rogers, Farnborough College of Technology. Chris Gozzard, Whitby Community College. Margaret Emson, Exeter College. Gina Barrs, City & Islington College, London. Harvey Cole at Huddersfield New College. Jean Frodsham, Bury College. Francis Nicholson and Helen Dean, Amersham & Wycombe College. Barry Brookes, Castle Community School, Deal. Sarah Perman at the TUC. Peter Clark at the CBI, and Rowena Hughes at the CBI National Manufacturing Council. Jess Enderby at UCAS.

And of course to all the students who have been the early graduates of the GNVQs.

*Janet Gibson*
*London, 1996*

# Introduction

*'A person with a GNVQ has qualifications to
continue studying and skills to start work.'*
N A D Carey, Director General,
City & Guilds of London Institute

---

### CHAPTER SUMMARY

This chapter gives a broad overview of GNVQs and explains:

- ▶ why GNVQs were introduced
- ▶ vocational qualifications as part of the national framework of qualifications
- ▶ the equal status of GNVQs with GCSEs and A levels
- ▶ the National Council of Vocational Qualifications
- ▶ the awarding bodies
- ▶ the vocational areas.

---

## WHAT IS A GNVQ?

It is a new *vocational* qualification. This means that the qualification is work-related. It is concerned with the general skills and knowledge needed within an occupation, profession or trade. The initials stand for General National Vocational Qualification. GNVQs are broad-based across a vocational area and are not related to one particular job.

'We are glad now that we did a GNVQ because it opened our eyes to the wider view of the vocational area and to the range of skills needed to be successful.'

Kate, Leisure & Tourism GNVQ
Tom, Art & Design GNVQ

7

GNVQs have not replaced those vocational courses that teach about specific areas of employment; there are many of these, ranging from agriculture and aboriculture to water treatment.

# WHO IS IT FOR?

The GNVQ is aimed mainly at 16–19 year old full-time students, although schools are beginning to offer part of the programme to 14 year olds. At advanced level the qualification is an alternative to GCE A levels. It is also for older students who wish to return to study. GNVQs are one part of the new national vocational qualifications framework. In 1995, 44,781 students completed a GNVQ course and gained a full award.

Chapter 9 'GNVQ Achievements' includes stories from students who have taken a GNVQ course. You can read about why they did a GNVQ, what they studied, what they thought about the course, and what they have gone on to do.

# GNVQs AND NVQs

GNVQs are mostly studied at school or college and have a broad base of study (that's why they've been called 'general'). In addition to GNVQs, another set of vocational qualifications have been introduced which are aimed at people in employment. These are called NVQs (National Vocational Qualifications). NVQs are job-focused and can be gained by people at their place of work, based on the work they do. GNVQs and NVQs together are described as the National Vocational Qualifications Framework.

GNVQs and NVQs apply to England, Wales and Northern Ireland. Scotland has introduced GSVQs (General Scottish Vocational Qualifications) and SVQs (Scottish Vocational Qualifications); see Chapter 6.

# WHY GNVQs?

For a very long time it has been argued that there should be an alternative to the traditional academic GCE A levels. We know that A levels do not suit everyone, and they do not prepare people for work. Other countries, like France and Germany, have broad courses of study for 16 year olds rather than the study of single subjects in depth.

The aim of GNVQs is to introduce high-quality work-related courses with the same status as academic qualifications.

'The manufacturing course is an excellent alternative to A level. It covers a wide variety of skills and topics, is work-related, and provides good links with industries in the community.'
Matthew, a 2nd year Advanced Manufacturing GNVQ student

By choosing the GNVQ course for the area of work you would like to do, you will learn the skills and knowledge to prepare you for employment in that vocational area. The qualification will also be recognized for entry to further and higher education if you want to continue your studies.

## GNVQ LEVELS

Currently, GNVQs are available at three levels for those aged 16 or over:

| | Vocational | | | Academic |
|---|---|---|---|---|
| | NVQ | GNVQ | | equivalent |
| Level 1 = | NVQ 1 = | Foundation | = | 4 GCSEs D–G grades |
| Level 2 = | NVQ 2 = | Intermediate | = | 4 GCSEs A–C grades |
| Level 3 = | NVQ 3 = | Advanced | = | 2 A levels |

**Table 1** Levels of study post-16

## GNVQ PART ONE AT KEY STAGE 4

In a limited number of schools at present, some of the GNVQ units – offered as Part One GNVQ – are available to students at age 14 as part of the national curriculum at Key Stage 4. This is to give students in Year 10 a choice of vocational as well as academic subjects. Students will still have to study the mandatory academic subjects, but now students can choose a vocational pathway at 14. The Part One GNVQ will be a qualification in its own right, and will be accepted as credits towards the full GNVQ.

There will be two levels of GNVQ at Key Stage 4:

| Level | Academic equivalent |
|-------|---------------------|
| Foundation Part One | 2 GCSEs D–G grades |
| Intermediate Part One | 2 GCSEs A–C grades |

**Table 2** Levels of study at age 14

# NATIONAL FRAMEWORK OF QUALIFICATIONS

The 'national framework of qualifications' brings together NVQs, GNVQs and academic qualifications as the three main qualification choices in the UK. It means that the vocational qualifications and the academic qualifications have equal status within the education system.

The framework gives you choices in how you gain those important qualifications. To reach the same level of education you can choose a vocational route or an academic route – or a mix. Qualifications relate to each other by their level, rather like being located on the rung of a ladder (see Table 3).

'I was sponsored on my Advanced Manufacturing GNVQ course and that would have been sufficient for employment with my sponsor, but I decided to widen my studies so I took an additional GNVQ unit in electrical principles for manufacturing, and an AS level in Chemistry.'

Matthew

'I knew I wanted to be a primary school teacher. In the first year of study for 2 A levels I took the opportunity to add Intermediate GNVQ in Health & Social Care. I enjoyed this so much that in the second year I took six units of the Advanced GNVQ in Health & Social Care which gave me the equivalence of a third A level.'

Jennie

Because the qualifications have equal status at each level, you can choose which qualification to take at each level.

| | |
|---|---|
| **Level 4** ↑ | part Degree<br>GNVQ4*<br>NVQ4 |
| **Level 3** | A level<br>Advanced GNVQ<br>NVQ3 |
| **Level 2** | GCSE [A–C grades]<br>Intermediate GNVQ<br>NVQ2 |
| **Level 1** | GCSE [D–G grades]<br>Foundation GNVQ<br>NVQ1 |
| Part One | National Curriculum. Key Stage 4 |

**Table 3** Broad equivalence of levels of academic and vocational qualifications
* Consideration of a level 4 GNVQ is still taking place

# THE NATIONAL COUNCIL FOR VOCATIONAL QUALIFICATIONS (NCVQ)

The National Council for Vocational Qualifications was established to develop and implement a comprehensive system of vocational qualifications. It has overall responsibility for GNVQs and NVQs.

The Council authorizes examination boards to be an official 'Vocational Awarding Body'. It then approves and monitors the qualifications they administer to ensure they meet national standards of quality and consistency.

# VOCATIONAL AWARDING BODIES

These are the examination boards which have been accredited to offer GNVQs. Currently there are three awarding bodies: the Business & Technology Education Council (BTEC); City & Guilds of London Institute (C&G); and the Royal Society of Arts (RSA).

# GNVQs – BROAD-BASED AND FLEXIBLE

Students on GNVQ courses are offered a broad vocational programme of study. GNVQ courses are modular – that is they are made up of units of study. A set number of units (depending on the level) must be taken to be awarded the full qualification. The total number is made up of compulsory units plus others that you choose. You can also take 'additional units' at advanced level.

Each unit is assessed and certificated separately. Once you have passed a unit, you are credited with that unit. You continue to accumulate credits until you have a credit for each of the units making up the qualification. There is no time limit on achieving the full number of units. The awarding bodies recognize each others' certificates, and they have units in common. So if you are not able to follow the full course of study in one go, or if your study is interrupted, you will not have lost the units you passed. You can complete the qualification, perhaps even with a different awarding body, when you are able to pick up your studies again.

In case you are wondering whether credits in GNVQ can be used towards an NVQ or an A level, remember that the three qualifications are each designed to meet different needs. There may be some overlap between GNVQ and NVQ but generally they are different in nature and scope. At the moment a national credit transfer framework between the three qualifications has not been developed.

# GNVQ VOCATIONAL AREAS

GNVQ began its second year in September 1994. 10,000 courses were run in over 2,000 schools and colleges for 150,000 students aged from 14 to over 50.

For September 1995, ten different vocational areas are available at foundation, intermediate and advanced levels. Five more are in planning, three of which are being piloted now. Table 4 shows the introduction and availability of GNVQs at foundation level, and Table 5 the availability of GNVQs at intermediate and advanced levels.

| Course area | 1994–5 | 1995–6 | 1996–7 | 1997–8 |
|---|---|---|---|---|
| Art & Design | restricted** | √ | √ | √ |
| Business | restricted** | √ | √ | √ |
| Construction & the Built Environment | pilot | √ | √ | √ |
| Engineering | pilot | √ | √ | √ |
| Health & Social Care | restricted** | √ | √ | √ |
| Hospitality & Catering | pilot | √ | √ | √ |
| Information Technology | pilot | √ | √ | √ |
| Leisure & Tourism | restricted** | √ | √ | √ |
| Manufacturing | restricted** | √ | √ | √ |
| Science | pilot | √ | √ | √ |
| Landbased & Environmental Industries | | | (pilot)* | |
| Media: Communication & Production | | | (pilot)* | |
| Performing Arts | | | (pilot)* | |
| Retail & Distributive Services | | | (pilot)* | |

**Table 4** GNVQ vocational areas at Foundation level

*possible introduction; **restricted take-up (both are mainly limited to those centres offering Intermediate GNVQs in the same vocational area)

| Course area | 1994–5 | 1995–6 | 1996–7 | 1997–8 |
|---|---|---|---|---|
| Art & Design | √ | √ | √ | √ |
| Business | √ | √ | √ | √ |
| Construction & the Built Environment | √ | √ | √ | √ |
| Engineering | pilot | √ | √ | √ |
| Health & Social Care | √ | √ | √ | √ |
| Hospitality & Catering | √ | √ | √ | √ |
| Information Technology | pilot | √ | √ | √ |
| Leisure & Tourism | √ | √ | √ | √ |
| Manufacturing | √ | √ | √ | √ |
| Science | √ | √ | √ | √ |
| | | | | |
| Management Studies (Advanced only) | pilot | pilot | √ | √ |
| Media: Communication & Production | pilot | pilot | √ | √ |
| Retail & Distributive Services | pilot | pilot | √ | √ |
| Landbased & Environmental Industries | | | pilot | |
| Performing Arts | | | pilot | |

**Table 5** GNVQ vocational areas at Intermediate and Advanced levels

## GNVQ Part One vocational areas

At Key Stage 4, Part One programmes are being piloted in selected schools in three vocational areas:

Business
Health & Social Care
Manufacturing

# 1

# What is a GNVQ?

**CHAPTER SUMMARY**

This chapter explains:

▶ the modular structure of GNVQs
▶ how units make up a programme of study
▶ recognition between the three awarding bodies
▶ accreditation and certification
▶ levels of study
▶ the Part One GNVQ for school students at age 14.

What both sides of industry (the TUC and the CBI) say about GNVQs:

'GNVQs make useful connections between education and industry and they enable students to master broad skills which will be valuable to them in their working lives.'
John Monks, General Secretary, Trades Union Congress

'GNVQs work for young people'
Howard Davies, Director-General (1992–95),
Confederation of British Industry

When you have completed compulsory schooling at the age of 16, you are free to choose either to find employment or continue your studies. But if any of the statements below describe you, then a GNVQ may be just what you are looking for:

- I want to be better qualified to get a good job and improve my career prospects.
- I didn't do so well at GCSEs, but want to improve my qualifications.
- I could go on to A levels, but I would prefer a more practical course at the same level and status.
- I want a course that will give me the option of going to university.
- I have been working and already have some knowledge and experience. I would like recognition for this, and to add to it to gain a qualification.
- I may have to interrupt my studies. I therefore want a course that will credit me for the work I do and then allow me to complete my studies for the full qualification when I am able.
- I want a course that will increase my job prospects and widen opportunities.
- School was ok, but . . . I want to achieve and I can work hard. I need a course that gives me more responsibility and a different style of working and learning.

## A POST-16 QUALIFICATION

GNVQs are on offer to students at Year 12, with a limited offer available at Year 10 (Part One GNVQ at Key Stage 4 – see 'Levels, Part One GNVQ' at the end of this chapter, and Chapter 2). They are also available to *anyone* over the age of 16 wishing to follow a vocational course of study. So there is no upper age limit. If you study at a college there may be mature students on the programmes, either full-time or part-time. This would be a plus, as all students usually find many advantages from a mixed age range course.

What is new is that you will be credited with each GNVQ unit you pass, and there is no time limit on achieving all the units for a full GNVQ qualification.

## LENGTH OF COURSE

Where courses are offered on a full-time basis, Foundation and Intermediate level courses are generally for one year, and Advanced level courses for two years.

Part One GNVQs can be taken by 14–16 year olds, and will be studied alongside GCSEs in Years 10 and 11.

# A MODULAR COURSE

The GNVQ programmes cover a wide range of work-related areas for you to choose from. Each programme offers a broad base of learning within an occupational area, by grouping together related areas of study in that occupational area. Each area of study is known as a 'unit', and units are put together to make up the qualification. This method of putting together a course is called 'modular'. There are *mandatory* units, *optional* units, and *additional* units.

'I want to travel abroad and work as an air hostess or a courier. The GNVQ opened my eyes to the range of skills needed to be successful in tourism.'

Jessica, Advanced Leisure and Tourism GNVQ student

The vocational areas and the units are listed in Chapter 3, 'The GNVQ Courses'.

It is important to stress that whilst GNVQ programmes are preparation for employment and have a more practical approach than GCSEs and A levels, they are nonetheless as academically rigorous. They have been designed to be of equal standing.

## Mandatory and optional units

Within each occupational area, there will be units you must study. These are the 'mandatory' units. In addition, there will be a list of units from which you make a choice to make up the total number of units for the course. These are the 'optional' units. (Some students find this term confusing because they are not 'optional' in that you have a choice of whether to take them or not! You must study units from the optional list.)

## Additional units – enhancing your qualification

You can if you wish, add extra units to your programme of study. 'Additional units' are therefore over and above the units required for the full qualification. The additional units can be chosen from those designed for the specific occupational area you are following, or from any other GNVQ programme. You can also add-on NVQ units.

These units may be added to suit your needs, either because a unit subject interests you and you want to expand your knowledge, or because it would enhance your qualification, or because it would be a requirement for employment or university.

> 'I studied Advanced Art & Design GNVQ, but enhanced this with a vocational certificate in Aerobics. I am now taking a BA degree in Sports Studies and Art.'
>
> Heather

# CORE SKILLS

Core skills are defined as skills which are 'required in a wide range of occupations and life in general'. That is why they are called 'core', ie at the heart of what we need to be able to do.

To achieve a GNVQ, you will need to show competence in three core skills areas:

- Communications
- Application of number
- Information technology

These three core skills units are part of each GNVQ, but they vary in difficulty according to the level of study.

Core skills are not assessed as individual units. You develop these skills within the work you do on the programme. So you will find these skills assessed as part of the work and activities you do. The focus of assessment of core skills is on your ability to *use* these skills.

You may find that if your skills are already well developed, you will be encouraged to achieve core skills at a higher level than the course you are on.

You will not find English and maths taught separately on a GNVQ programme because the emphasis is on 'integration'. However, schools and colleges often provide workshops for students who need help in developing these areas. If your plan is to go on to university and you do not have a good GCSE in English and maths, do check whether the university will require you to have one or both. I would point out that one of the awarding bodies strongly advises against GNVQ programmes having links with GCSE English, maths and computer studies. Some universities, and employers, who have exercised caution or followed tradition by asking for GCSE maths have dropped this requirement when they have understood the maths element of Advanced GNVQ programmes (see Chapter 9, 'GNVQ Achievements').

## ADDITIONAL PERSONAL SKILLS UNITS

There are two more skills units which you can add-on to your qualification. These are:

- Working with others
- Improving own learning and performance

Problem-solving skills additional units are also available, but they are not yet approved for accreditation and certificates will not be awarded. You can record your achievement of the Problem Solving unit in your National Record of Achievement.

## THREE DIFFERENT AWARDING BODIES – THREE DIFFERENT OFFERS?

The National Council for Vocational Qualifications determines the vocational programme areas and the units of study within each. The three awarding bodies (BTEC, C&G and RSA) implement the programmes and award the qualification.

The mandatory units in each vocational programme area, and the core skills units, will be the same regardless of the awarding body. But, as the awarding bodies are allowed to devise their own optional and additional units, the total programme offer will vary according to the awarding body.

When you have chosen the programme area you want to follow you will then choose where to study. Each institution offering GNVQ programmes will use one of the three awarding bodies. You should find out which one before you finally enrol.

It's a good idea to find out what units each awarding body makes available. Then check with the education establishments which awarding body they use, and which of those optional and additional units they can offer to students. The choice of units available to you will depend on the size of the GNVQ programme offered at the centre and the expertise available among its staff.

# CREDIT ACCUMULATION

This is definitely the best bit! GNVQs are not like other qualifications where if you don't finish the course you lose recognition for what you *did* pass. With GNVQs, you are credited with each unit as you pass it. Whilst the majority of students will follow a programme of study through to completion, every student will receive a certificate listing the units they have achieved.

A-level students, for example, can take advantage of this by taking some vocational units to broaden their study (see Chapter 9, 'GNVQ Achievements').

'I am very good at karate, and through this I became very, very interested in Japan. While I was on the Advanced Leisure & Tourism course, the possibility to go to Japan became real and I leapt at it. This was an opportunity I couldn't let pass. Although it meant I would not be able to finish the course, I do have the certificates for all the units of the course I completed. It is always open to me to complete the remaining units for the full qualification.'

John

The Certificate of Unit Credit is issued by the awarding body offering the qualification, and credits are accumulated for the award of a full GNVQ – regardless of the time taken.

# ACCREDITATION OF PRIOR LEARNING (APL)

This is mainly of benefit to older students who are returning to study. If you can produce evidence that you are already competent in parts of the syllabus, you will be credited with those competences. So if you have been at work and you can prove you can already do aspects of the work required on the course to the standard required by the level of study, this will count towards the qualification.

# LEVELS – GNVQ

Three levels have so far been developed. Each level will state a number of mandatory and optional units for the full qualification. At each level the three core skills units must also be taken.

*Level 1 – Foundation*    As the name suggests this is the lowest level. It is for students with no previous qualifications. Six vocational units are studied – three mandatory and three optional units. The difference at this level is that students have the opportunity to choose the three optional units from other vocational areas. There are nine units in total (six + three core skills). It will probably take one year to complete the qualification.

*Level 2 – Intermediate*    This level has equivalence with GCSE level. Within the occupational area chosen, six vocational units must be taken. There are nine units in total (six + three core skills). The qualification will probably take one year to complete, and is equivalent to four GCSE passes at grade A-C.

*Level 3 – Advanced*    This level has equivalence with GCSE A level. GNVQ Advanced is also known as the 'vocational A level', and is the equivalent to two A level passes. Within the occupational area chosen, 12 vocational units must be studied at this level, making 15 units in total (twelve + three core skills). The period of study will normally be two years.

Levels 4 and 5 have not yet been developed. In the meantime, for example, BTEC are continuing to offer their Higher National Diploma in all subjects until GNVQ4 is available. Level 5 will represent professional qualifications.

# LEVELS – PART ONE GNVQ

Part One GNVQ for 14–16 year olds is not yet widely available, but is offered at two levels. It is a stand-alone qualification, but as the units are the same as those which make up the full qualification at the same level, it goes towards that full GNVQ post-16.

*Foundation Part One* This is for students who would like to take vocational options in Year 10 perhaps as a preparation for employment or further vocational study. Six units are studied from the Foundation level GNVQ – three vocational units and the three level 1 core skills units. The vocational areas available are Business, Health & Social Care, and Manufacturing. Successful completion of the six units will result in a Foundation Part One Certificate which is equivalent to two GCSEs grades D–G.

*Intermediate Part One* This is a vocational option for students who want a work-related element as part of their studies at 14 before proceeding to A levels, a full Intermediate GNVQ or the Advanced GNVQ (or a combination of academic and vocational qualifications), or into employment. Six units are studied from the Intermediate level GNVQ – three vocational units and the three level 2 core skills units. The vocational areas available are Business, Health & Social Care, and Manufacturing. Successful completion of the six units will result in an Intermediate Part One Certificate which is equivalent to two GCSEs grades A–C.

**2**

# The GNVQ Programme – How it Works

*'If I had my time again, I would certainly choose the
GNVQ route of study'*
a British Rail Manager

---

### CHAPTER SUMMARY

This chapter explains:

- ▶ how a GNVQ vocational unit is structured
- ▶ the terminology used in GNVQs
- ▶ assessment and grading
- ▶ external tests
- ▶ going on to higher education
- ▶ Part One GNVQs at Key Stage 4
- ▶ the GNVQ Scholarship Scheme.

---

# STRUCTURE

## A Modular programme

So you are now going to embark on a GNVQ programme, and you have selected one of the vocational areas to study. In the previous chapter we learned that at every level it will be a modular programme, with:

- mandatory vocational units
- optional vocational units
- plus three mandatory core skills units.

Let's remind ourselves of how the units combine to meet the requirements for a GNVQ.

| Level | Mandatory Vocational Units | Optional Vocational Units | Mandatory Core Skills Units | Total units for A Full GNVQ |
|---|---|---|---|---|
| Foundation | 3 | 3 | 3 | 9 |
| Intermediate | 4 | 2 | 3 | 9 |
| Advanced | 8 | 4 | 3 | 15 |

**Table 2.1** The GNVQ Modular programme

## Mandatory units

These units set out the fundamental skills, knowledge and understanding to be learned at each level.

## Optional units

These are further units of study within the occupational area which can take you into areas of specialization.

## Core skills units

The skills of communication, application of number, and information technology – the skills which are considered to be essential to work and life in general.

When you select your optional units, you can broaden your studies or take units that give you the opportunity to specialize towards a particular sector of the vocational area. The following, taken from BTEC, is an example of two of the pathways through the occupational area of Business – for those who are interested in accounting or marketing:

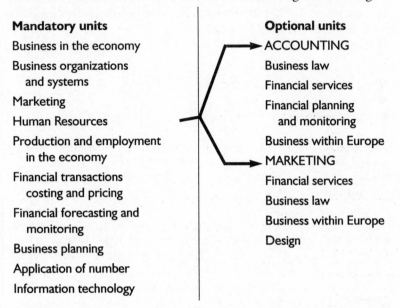

| Mandatory units | Optional units |
|---|---|
| Business in the economy | ACCOUNTING |
| Business organizations and systems | Business law |
| | Financial services |
| Marketing | Financial planning and monitoring |
| Human Resources | |
| Production and employment in the economy | Business within Europe |
| | MARKETING |
| Financial transactions costing and pricing | Financial services |
| | Business law |
| Financial forecasting and monitoring | Business within Europe |
| Business planning | Design |
| Application of number | |
| Information technology | |

**Table 2.2** Example of two possible pathways on a BTEC Business GNVQ

## The structure of a unit

The curriculum for each unit is divided into topics of study. Each topic, or 'Element' as it is called, specifies what you have to learn and do under headings of 'Performance Criteria', 'Range' and 'Evidence indicators'. So for each unit:

- there will be a number of Elements
- each Element will specify:
  - Performance criteria
  - Range
  - Evidence indicators.

This is all explained in this chapter.

'I hadn't done well at GCSEs. GNVQs opened up a real opportunity to achieve. I loved the course and managed to achieve a Distinction at Intermediate and Advanced levels. It's put me on the road to be really successful'

Deborah, GNVQ Intermediate and Advanced Business student

# CONTENT

In GNVQs the course of study is quite specific. You are told:

- what particular aspects of the subject area you must cover and to what depth
- what practical work you must do to demonstrate your knowledge and ability.

If this is the first time you have looked at the GNVQ curriculum, you will probably find the terminology quite daunting. Hopefully, this chapter will simplify it for you. But don't worry too much now as schools and colleges will spend time at the beginning of the course, the Induction period, to help you become familiar with the structure and terminology. It will be essential that you understand the curriculum and the work you are required to do so that you can build your portfolio of evidence which will be assessed by the external verifier.

To understand how a GNVQ works, let's take Intermediate GNVQ in Leisure and Tourism as an example. We'll take it step-by-step.

Vocational area: *Leisure and Tourism*

Level: *Intermediate*

## Units

Each vocational area is made up of a number of units of study. At Intermediate level, you will study nine units for a full award. For Leisure and Tourism you must take the four mandatory Leisure and Tourism units plus any two units from the optional units list for Leisure and Tourism. (You will obviously go for the units that appeal to you and towards areas in which you would like to specialize.) You will also be assessed against the three mandatory core skill units at level 2.

'Before I did the GNVQ, I hadn't realised what a narrow view I had of Leisure & Tourism. It gave me the opportunity to cover a wide area of study.'

Sabia

We are now this far into the structure and into the programme:

Vocational area:     *Leisure and Tourism*

Level:     *Intermediate*

Units:     *Four Mandatory*

1. Investigating the leisure and tourism industries (Intermediate)
2. Marketing and promoting leisure and tourism products (Intermediate)
3. Customer service in leisure and tourism (Intermediate)
4. Contributing to the running of an event (Intermediate)

*Two Optional (probably from a list of four) – for example:*

- Health and safety in leisure and tourism (Intermediate)
- Investigating the UK tourism industry (Intermediate)
- Investigating sports and recreation (Intermediate)
- Researching tourist destinations (Intermediate)

*Three Core Skills*

- Communication (Level 2)
- Application of number (Level 2)
- Information technology (Level 2)

## Elements

We now have the nine units for Leisure and Tourism. If we then look at each unit we find it is broken down into more defined areas for the student to look at in more detail. The term used to describe these more clearly defined areas is 'Element'.

Each unit will be made up of between two to five Elements.

We'll take one mandatory, one optional and one core skills unit to learn a little more about the Elements of the curriculum.

*Mandatory unit 1: Investigating the leisure and tourism industries (Intermediate)*
(this is broken down into three parts or 'Elements'):

| | |
|---|---|
| Element 1.1 | Investigate the leisure and recreation industry nationally and locally |
| Element 1.2 | Investigate the travel and tourism industry nationally and locally |
| Element 1.3 | Prepare for employment in the leisure and tourism industries |

*Optional unit: Investigating sports and recreations (Intermediate)*
(this is broken down into three parts or 'Elements'):

| | |
|---|---|
| Element 1 | Explain the importance of recreational activities to participants |
| Element 2 | Investigate the use of sports and recreational facilities |
| Element 3 | Plan sports and recreational activities |

*Core Skills: Communication (Level 2)*
(this is broken down into four parts or 'Elements')

| | |
|---|---|
| Element 2.1 | Take part in discussions |
| Element 2.2 | Produce written material |
| Element 2.3 | Use images |
| Element 2.4 | Read and respond to written materials |

We will now look at the elements in more detail.

There are between two and five Elements for each unit which give more information on what the curriculum is to cover. Each Element is seen as a specific area of study, and it is here that the depth and breadth of study is made clear.

The work you produce for assessment will be based upon what is required for each Element, which is detailed under the headings of 'Performance Criteria', 'Range', and 'Evidence Indicators' (see Figure 1).

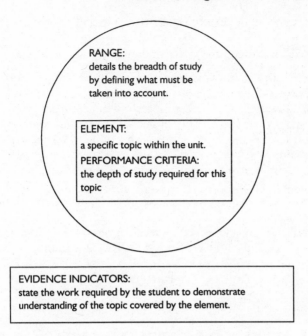

RANGE:
details the breadth of study by defining what must be taken into account.

ELEMENT:
a specific topic within the unit.
PERFORMANCE CRITERIA:
the depth of study required for this topic

EVIDENCE INDICATORS:
state the work required by the student to demonstrate understanding of the topic covered by the element.

**Figure 2.1** The composition of an element

To understand the composition of an Element, I will use as an example the first Element of unit 1 (and therefore numbered 1.1) of Intermediate Leisure and Tourism (see Figure 2.1).

**Q. If you were asked to describe leisure and recreation in the UK, how well do you think you could do? How many facilities, products, services and locations could you list and describe?**

As explained on page 25, each element will specify Performance Criteria, Range and Evidence Indicators. For Element 1.1 of Intermediate Leisure and Tourism, these are as follows.

Element 1.1: Investigate the leisure and recreation industry nationally and locally

# Performance Criteria

A student must:

- Describe the **main components** of the leisure and recreation industry in the UK.
- Give an example of a facility for each of the **main components.**
- **Compare** the characteristics of public, private and voluntary sectors in the leisure and recreation industry, supporting the comparison with examples.
- Give examples of leisure and recreation **products and services** available nationally.
- Give examples of leisure and recreation **facilities of national significance.**
- Describe leisure and recreation facilities, products and services available in a locality and give **reasons for their location.**

# Range

Six aspects under Range are listed for Element 1.1. The first three are:

- **Main components**: arts and entertainment, sports and physical activities, outdoor activities, heritage, play, catering and accommodation.
- **Facilities**: theatres, halls, tracks, museums, parks, sports centres, swimming pools, activity centres, heritage sites, play areas, catering provision, accommodation provision, natural environment features with leisure potential.
- **Compare** on the basis of: scale of operation (national, local), who undertakes the work (paid staff, volunteers, combination of both), method of funding (grants, membership fees, profit/surplus, subsidy).

# Evidence indicators

A brief report outlining in general terms the leisure and recreation industry nationally. The report should:

- Describe the main components of the leisure and recreation industry, supported by examples of six facilities – one for each main component.
- Compare the characteristics of the public, private and voluntary sectors of the industry on the basis of the three criteria listed in the

range 'Compare'. The comparison should be supported by examples of three facilities – one from each sector.
■ Give examples of leisure and recreation products and services available nationally. Sufficient examples should be given to cover, in broad terms, the range for 'Products and services'.
■ Give four examples of leisure and recreation facilities – one for each of the main range categories.

# SUMMARY OF STRUCTURE AND CONTENT

Elements make up units, and units make up the Programme. The *Range* describes what specific aspects have to be addressed for each Element of the curriculum. *Performance Criteria* tell you in what depth you need to work and the *Evidence Indicators* the work you need to do.

| | |
|---|---|
| Vocational area | the occupational area of the programme |
| Level | the GNVQ programme level |
| Units | the mandatory and optional modules which combine to make up the GNVQ programme |
| Elements | more detailed information and explanation of the curriculum for each unit |
| Performance Criteria | describe the depth of study to be under taken (performance criteria are given for each element) |
| Range | indicate the breadth of study by identifying the particular aspects of the industry or service area which the student must understand (the range is stipulated for each element) |
| Evidence Indicators | a paragraph explaining what is required of the student to attain a pass mark for an element. |

**Table 2.3** Summary of the GNVQ structure and content

# ASSESSMENT AND GRADING

## Assessment

### Units

Each Element of a unit is assessed through assignments or projects and it is recorded whether you have achieved or still have to achieve an Element. You need to achieve all of the Elements in each unit to be awarded a pass in that Unit. If you do not achieve an Element, you will have the opportunity to retake it during the programme. The assignment front sheet or other record sheet will identify the Element and the Performance Criteria for each unit covered by the assignment – for the vocational Units and the core skills units. You may also find that assignments are integrated, that is requiring you to bring together learning across Units to undertake one project.

At the same time as your work is assessed, you will be given feedback on the standard of your work against the grading criteria which are used to determine whether you can be awarded a Merit or Distinction. This feedback will be recorded as 'interim grading indications'.

Assessment is carried out by vocational assessors and internal verifiers in the centre where you are studying, and by external verifiers appointed by the Awarding Body.

### Core skills

The work you produce for the vocational Elements will integrate the core skills. For example, an assignment may require you to:

- use a computer to produce a report on tourism
- write using the appropriate tone
- form well-constructed sentences
- present your findings in a logical order
- include calculations.

The core skills are assessed by how well you compile and present the report.

With core skills, however, levels can be awarded at the level of the course or, if your skills are at a higher level, awarded accordingly. For example, if you are following an Intermediate level course, core skills could be awarded at levels 2, 3 or 4.

## Portfolio of Evidence

Every student must put together a Portfolio of Evidence. This is a collection of the work you have done which provides the evidence that you have met all the requirements of the Unit specifications for a GNVQ. You will include in your Portfolio projects, assignments and other activities you have carried out as part of the course. It will also include your externally set test results. An important part of the Portfolio will be evidence relating to the grading criteria – which shows how you approached and carried out the assignment work. This will include your individual action plans.

The following is an example of an action plan developed by a student for a project looking into access to health and care services (Element 4.2) for the Intermediate Health & Social Care GNVQ:

### Action Plan (for weeks 4 and 5)

| Action | Evidence | PC/Range | Timescale | Resources | Adjustment to plan |
|---|---|---|---|---|---|
| Read leaflets. Talk to Mr L to find out more about health and care workers. | list of different health and care workers who support family | Element 4.2 PC2 All range | By Tuesday (talk to Mr L on Friday). | DSS leaflets. Mr L and tutor. | Mr L not in on Friday. Spoke to him on Monday. |
| Find out more about the roles of health and care workers on the list | Descriptions of peoples jobs – what they do, responsibilities, who they work for. | Element 4.2 PC2 All range | After Tuesday when list ready. | Library books, DSS leaflets, notes taken when speakers come to college. | |
| Look in detail at social work – what I'm most interested in – talk to JH and book more library time. | Exploration of social work – different types, what social workers do, job descriptions. | Element 4.2 PC2 Social workers | Ring JH as soon as poss and by 28th. | JH, library books on social work, what I know from placement | Library book I needed was out. Went to local library instead. |

**Figure 2.2** An Action Plan – example from Health & Social Care

This student demonstrated her ability to break down an activity into manageable tasks. She planned the best order in which to carry out tasks (filling in the 'timescale' in each case), but recognized that the tasks were interdependent and adjusted her plan accordingly.

The final award of a GNVQ depends on the production of the Portfolio as it is part of the final evaluation.

## Grading

For a full GNVQ, you can be awarded one of three grades:

- pass,
- merit, or
- distinction.

The GNVQ grading criteria determine the grade of your final award. Because GNVQs are designed to encourage an active approach to learning, the grading criteria focus on your performance. That is:

- how you tackle the work
- how much responsibility you take for planning your work
- how you decide what information you need
- how well you review and evaluate your performance
- the overall quality of your work.

## Grading themes

The grading criteria are grouped into four themes, which are shown in Table 2.4.

## Pass grade

To obtain a pass grade you must successfully complete all the required units: nine for a Foundation or Intermediate GNVQ; 15 for an Advanced GNVQ. This means you will have shown you know and understand the whole of the GNVQ and you will have:

- shown evidence in your portfolio which satisfies all the element requirements; and
- passed any externally-set tests.

## Merit and distinction grades

To be awarded a merit or distinction you will have met the requirements for a pass grade, but in addition *one third or more* of your evi-

|  | Foundation and Intermediate Criteria | Advanced Criteria |
|---|---|---|
| **Theme 1: Planning** | 1. Drawing up plans of action<br>2. Monitoring courses of action | 1. Drawing up plans of action<br>2. Monitoring courses of action |
| **Theme 2: Information seeking and information handling** | 3. Identifying information needs<br><br>4. Identifying and using sources to obtain information | 3. Identifying and using sources to obtain information<br>4. Establishing the validity of information |
| **Theme 3 Evaluation** | 5. Evaluating outcomes and justifying approaches | 5. Evaluating outcomes and alternatives<br>6. Justifying particular approaches to tasks/activity |
| **Theme 4 Quality of outcomes** | 6. Synthesis<br>7. Command of 'language'* | 7. Synthesis<br>8. Command of 'language'* |

**Table 2.4** The GNVQ Grading Criteria

*'Language' refers to the concepts, forms of expression and presentation used within the GNVQ vocational area or discipline

dence will meet all the merit or distinction grading criteria. Core skills units are not graded and do not count towards merit or distinction.

The following shows what makes the difference between a merit and distinction for Criterion 1, *Drawing up plans of action*:

Criterion 1:
*Drawing up plans of action*

This criterion recognizes that planning skills play a crucial part in tackling work, and that planning is more difficult when students structure a complex activity themselves.

- **Merit** – Student *independently* draws up plans of action for a series of *discrete* tasks. The plans prioritize the different tasks within the given time period.

■ **Distinction** – Student *independently* draws up plans of action for *complex* activities. The plans prioritize the different tasks within the given time period.

The requirement that a third, and not all of your work, is required to meet the criteria for a merit or distinction is in recognition that you can't be expected to produce this standard of work with the first pieces of work you do.

*If you refer back to Figure 2.2, the Action Plan, the student received a Distinction for the project she was undertaking. She met the grading criteria 1–4 (planning, and information seeking and information handling).*

## Advanced GNVQ and A level grades

The grades of pass, merit and distinction at Advanced level are aligned to A level grades as follows:

| *Advanced GNVQ* | *A level* |
| --- | --- |
| Distinction | A/B |
| Merit | C |
| Pass | D/E |

# External tests

These are usually one hour, multiple-choice tests of 25–40 questions covering the unit curriculum. External tests can be sat at the end of the term in which the unit has been completed. Test results are given as 'Passed'; 'Not yet passed'; or 'within 10%' to indicate a pass was narrowly missed. A 70% pass mark is usually required. Externally set tests which are not passed can be resat during the programme, or in September for those students who have not completed their GNVQ in the previous academic year.

These tests are being reviewed and may become more varied in future.

# ENHANCING YOUR QUALIFICATION

## GNVQ/NVQ Units

You can enhance your GNVQ by taking additional units. The additional units you choose may be from the mandatory and/or optional units in other GNVQ vocational areas, or units specially written as additional units, or NVQ language and/or vocational units. There are additional core skills units of 'Personal Skills – improving own learning and performance', 'Personal Skills – working with others', and 'Problem Solving', but currently only Personal Skills are accredited.

The additional units available will depend on the centre and the awarding body. The awarding body issues specifications of additional units to colleges and schools so ask your centre for a list. Additional units are not externally tested.

## A and AS levels

The Advanced GNVQ – or 'vocational A level' – is designed to be at a comparable standard to GCSE A levels, so if you are taking an Advanced GNVQ, you can consider taking an A level or an AS level to enhance your qualification. Or alternatively, where A/AS levels are modular (usually six per A level) you may find opportunities here for more flexible learning.

Comparability between GNVQs and A levels means that six GNVQ units are equivalent to an A level, and three GNVQ units equivalent to an AS level:

| GNVQ units | GCE equivalent |
|:---:|:---:|
| 6 | A level |
| 3 | AS level |

The following are examples of additional studies some students decided to take. It shows the course they were following and their progression from the course.

**All you need to know about GNVQs**

| GNVQ course the student was on | Additional studies | Progressed to. . . |
|---|---|---|
| Business | 5 GNVQ units | employment with a major bank |
| Business | A level Sociology | American Studies degree |
| Business Leisure & Tourism | 3 GNVQ units French for Business GNVQ unit | European Business degree now Head Receptionist in a London hotel |
| Art & Design | Aerobics | Sports Studies & Art degree |
| Art & Design | GNVQ Health & Social Care units | Applied Art & Design degree |
| Health & Social Care | A level PE | Movement Studies degree |
| Manufacturing | 1 GNVQ unit, plus AS level Chemistry | employment with a major chemicals company |

# GNVQ SCHOLARSHIP SCHEME

This is a new initiative which the NCVQ has developed in partnership with leading employers, and is an opportunity for students to receive the backing and support of companies which are taking part in the scheme. Some of the participating companies which offer scholarships are:

- Vidal Sassoon, which offers scholarships open to Advanced and Intermediate students on Art & Design GNVQs;
- Girobank plc for Advanced Business students;
- McDonalds and the Post Office for Intermediate and Advanced Business students;
- Laing for Advanced Construction & the Built Environment students;
- The National Health Service Training Division for Advanced Health & Social Care students;
- Hilton Hotels for Hospitality & Catering students at Intermediate and Advanced level;
- United Biscuits for Intermediate and Advanced Manufacturing students.

The companies providing scholarships may additionally offer financial rewards, benefits in kind, or employment opportunities for GNVQ graduates. The details of the Scholarship Scheme will vary from company to company, and the scheme may not be available in all parts of the country.

# GNVQs AT KEY STAGE 4

Vocational qualifications are regarded as being of value to students of all levels of ability. It is now government policy that the National Curriculum will be reduced to allow vocational qualifications to be offered to students aged 14–16 years at Key Stage 4. The NCVQ is developing a Part One GNVQ for this age group which is currently being piloted in selected schools around the country. It is planned that in 1997, all students aged 14 will have vocational studies as part of the choices they can make in Year 10.

## GNVQ Part One

GNVQ Part One will be a qualification in its own right, and will be offered at Foundation and Intermediate levels. At both levels a total of six units will be taken: three vocational units and three core skills units.

| Level | Vocational units | Core skill units | Occupational areas | GCSE equivalent |
|-------|------------------|------------------|--------------------|-----------------|
| Foundation Level 1 | 3 units from Foundation level | 3 (level 1) | Business Health & Social Care Manufacturing | 2 additional GCSEs grades D–F |
| Intermediate Level 2 | 3 units from Intermediate level | 3 (level 2) | Business Health & Social Care Manufacturing | 2 additional GCSEs grades A–C |

**Table 2.5** Structure and academic equivalence of Part One GNVQ

The time required to study for this qualification will be equivalent to one day a week, or 20% of the Key Stage 4 timetable. GCSE mathematics will support attainment in the 'Application of number' core skills unit, and GCSE English will support Communication.

## Grading for Part One

To gain a pass grade at Part One, students must:

- demonstrate through their portfolio that they have achieved the performance criteria across the range and met the requirements of the evidence indicators;
- pass the mastery tests;
- demonstrate through their GCSE coursework and portfolio that they have met the three core skills units of Communication, Application of number and Information technology.

To gain a merit or distinction grade, students will have met the requirements for a pass grade and in addition must:

- demonstrate through their portfolio that they have met the requirements of the criteria within the grading themes. All students must complete a controlled assignment;
- gain an appropriate aggregate mark on the extension tests (which are in addition to the unit test).

# 3

# The GNVQ Courses

*'As a customer focused business, Network SouthCentral continually seek to improve the quality of staff we recruit to deal with customers. We find that those people with GNVQs have a better understanding of business and the importance of customers to a business.'*

Pam Gee, Station Manager
for 17 stations on Network SouthCentral

---

**CHAPTER SUMMARY**

This chapter explains:

►      how a programme is put together
►      the vocational programmes that are available
►      the mandatory and optional units at Foundation level,
         and flexibility of choice
►      the mandatory units at Intermediate and Advanced levels
►      the GNVQs that are being piloted, or are planned.

---

## BUILDING THE PROGRAMME

### Foundation level

At Foundation level only, all three awarding bodies (BTEC, G&G and RSA) offer the same mandatory and optional GNVQ units. This is designed to give you a greater flexibility of choice.

## All you need to know about GNVQs

You study the three mandatory units for the vocational area you enrol on. But the choice for your three optional units can be taken from any of the units offered at Foundation level, *whether mandatory or optional*, regardless of vocational area.

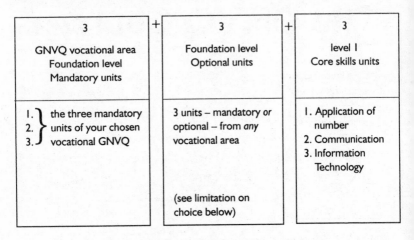

**Figure 3.1** Nine units for Foundation level

For example, if you enrolled on Foundation Business, to make up the six vocational units for study you may want to choose from the optional Business units, but you can also choose from the mandatory and optional units of Art & Design, Built Environment, or any of the other Foundation programmes' mandatory and optional units.

This gives you an opportunity to explore and experience different occupations, and will help you to decide what you would like to study at a higher level. The centre where you study will tell you what choices are available to you.

There are, however, two limitations on choice. Your combination of units must *not* include:

1.    more than two units beginning 'Investigating working in. . .'
2.    units with identical titles.

These are further explained in Table 3.1 and you will see they are fairly obvious.

| Mandatory unit 3: | *A maximum of two of these units may be chosen.* |
|---|---|
| You will notice that this unit always begins 'investigating working in. . .' | – so when you decide on your three options, only one can be 'unit 3' from another vocational area. |
| Common units:<br><br>There are some optional units which have been included in more than one vocational area, eg 'Contributing to a team activity', 'Health and Safety'. | *No two units with identical titles may be chosen:*<br>– when choosing your options, you cannot choose units of the same title even though they are from different vocational areas.<br><br><br>These 'common units' are marked with an asterisk (*) in the list for each vocational area. |

**Table 3.1** The two limitations on choice of units at Foundation level

## Intermediate and Advanced Level

### Mandatory, optional and additional units

At Intermediate and Advanced levels, the *mandatory* units will always be the same for GNVQs with the same title and level regardless of awarding body. Only the optional units vary because each awarding body is allowed to set their own. Your choice of optional units will be from those set by the awarding body *for the vocational area and level* you have enrolled on. Your final choice may be limited by what the school or college is able to offer.

Additional units can also be taken to enhance your qualification. The centre where you study will tell you what choices are available to you.

*Using the example of Accounting and Marketing pathways in BTEC GNVQs (see Chapter 2, p.25), the additional units for a student wishing to specialize further may be as shown in Table 3.2.*

## All you need to know about GNVQs

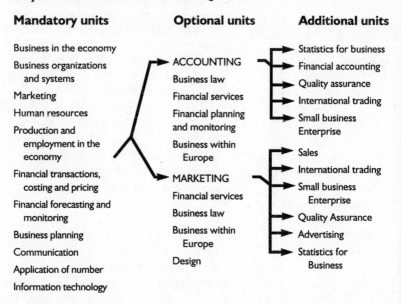

| Mandatory units | Optional units | Additional units |
|---|---|---|
| Business in the economy | | Statistics for business |
| Business organizations and systems | ACCOUNTING | Financial accounting |
| | Business law | Quality assurance |
| Marketing | Financial services | International trading |
| Human resources | Financial planning and monitoring | Small business Enterprise |
| Production and employment in the economy | Business within Europe | |
| | | Sales |
| Financial transactions, costing and pricing | MARKETING | International trading |
| | Financial services | Small business Enterprise |
| Financial forecasting and monitoring | Business law | Quality Assurance |
| | Business within Europe | Advertising |
| Business planning | Design | Statistics for Business |
| Communication | | |
| Application of number | | |
| Information technology | | |

**Table 3.2** Example of pathways on a BTEC Advanced GNVQ in Business

### Foreign Language Units

You will find in some vocational areas at Advanced level, foreign language units are included in the list of optional units. These follow the GNVQ model and deal with 'outcomes' and production of 'evidence'. The units on offer will relate to speaking and listening, ie 'Deal orally with varied daily activities', and 'Obtain information about non-routine and daily activities by listening'.

Foreign language units can also be taken as additional units. Reading and writing units are also available.

> 'I wanted to go on to do a European Business degree, so I chose a language unit in German as one of the optional units.'
> George, an Advanced Business student

### Core Skills Units

Every GNVQ programme includes three mandatory core skill units – Application of number; Communication; and Information technology. These three core skills units have been written for each level – not for each programme. Therefore, the units will be common to all

GNVQs at the same level irrespective of vocational area and awarding body.

A GNVQ programme will use the core skills units written for its level. The skills will be applied to the work of the vocational area.

# THE VOCATIONAL PROGRAMME AREAS

'The NMC wholeheartedly supports GNVQ Manufacturing as an effective way of teaching young people both core skills and life skills and sound practical knowledge of manufacturing in all its variations. Such skills and knowledge will be an important element in ensuring that the UK's manufacturing industries are able to compete with the world's best.'

The National Manufacturing Council
of the Confederation of British Industry (CBI)

The following are the vocational programmes offered as GNVQs. Except at Foundation level, only the mandatory units are listed. A full list of all the optional and additional units offered by each of the awarding bodies is too extensive to include here. Ultimately, what will be on offer to you will depend on where you study. As GNVQ programmes are monitored and updated, programme titles and unit titles may be subject to change.

(The 'common units' at Foundation level are marked with an asterisk (*). Units with the same title cannot be chosen twice.)

### ART AND DESIGN

The Art and Design programme is a broad course of study involving you in both creative activity ('art contexts') and how to work to a design brief ('design contexts'). You will be helped to develop your visual language into creative ideas through to the finished piece.

Through the levels you will develop skills, knowledge and understanding which will prepare you for entry into employment or self-employment in any art, craft or design sector; or further study.

## Foundation Art and Design

*Foundation mandatory units*
1. Exploring 2D techniques
2. Exploring 3D techniques
3. Investigating work in art, craft and design.

*Foundation optional units*
Three units are required for the full qualification. The list of Art and Design optional units is common to all the awarding bodies, but the choice also extends to the mandatory and optional units of any other Foundation programme.

4. Art, craft and design teamwork
5. Providing quality service to customers
6. Promotion and display
7. Designing a product
8. Carrying out an art or craft project
9. Investigating art, craft and design in other vocational areas.

*Core skills units at Level 1*
1. Application of number
2. Communication
3. Information Technology

## Intermediate Art and Design

*Intermediate mandatory units*
1. 2D Visual language
2. 3D Visual language
3. Exploring others' art, craft and design work
4. Applying the creative process

*Intermediate optional units*
Two optional units are required for the full qualification. The choice will depend upon the awarding body and what the centre offers where you study.

*Core skills units at Level 2*
1. Application of number
2. Communication
3. Information technology

## Advanced Art and Design

*Advanced mandatory units*
1. 2D Visual language
2. 3D Visual language
3. Working with media, materials and technology
4. Historical and contemporary contextual references
5. Business and professional practice
6. Working to self-identified art briefs
7. Working to set design briefs
8. Presenting work

*Advanced optional units*
Four optional units are required for the full qualification. The choice will depend upon the awarding body and what the centre offers where you study.

*Core skills units at Level 3*
1. Application of number
2. Communication
3. Information technology

**BUSINESS**

GNVQ Business is for any student who would like to work in administration or management. The programme introduces you to different types of organizations and will help you develop essential skills and knowledge in business through practical situations.

## Foundation Business

*Foundation mandatory units*
1. Processing business payments
2. Investigating business and customers
3. Investigating working in business

## All you need to know about GNVQs

*Foundation optional units*
Three units are required for the full qualification. The list of Business optional units is common to all the awarding bodies, but the choice also extends to the mandatory and optional units of any other Foundation programme.

4.* Contributing to a team activity
5.  Health and Safety in business
6.* Scheduling and booking
7.  Processing business information
8.  Providing office support
9.  Investigating employment

## Core skills units at Level 1

1.  Application of number
2.  Communication
3.  Information technology

## Intermediate Business

*Intermediate mandatory units*
1.  Business organizations and employment
2.  People in business organizations
3.  Consumers and customers
4.  Financial and administrative support

*Intermediate optional units*
Two optional units are required for the full qualification. The choice will depend upon the awarding body and what the centre offers where you study.

*Core skills units at Level 2*
1.  Application of number
2.  Communication
3.  Information technology

## Advanced Business

*Advanced mandatory units*
1.  Business in the economy
2.  Business organizations and systems
3.  Marketing
4.  Human resources

5. Production and employment in the economy
6. Financial transactions, costing and pricing
7. Financial forecasting and monitoring
8. Business planning

*Advanced optional units*
Four optional units are required for the full qualification. The choice will depend upon the awarding body and what the centre offers where you study.

*Core skills units at Level 3*
1. Application of number
2. Communication
3. Information technology

### Construction and the Built Environment

If you are interested in any aspect of the construction industry – perhaps design, surveying, civil engineering, construction technology, or architecture – this GNVQ covers not only the essential skills and knowledge, but also environmental considerations, materials and building structures.

## Foundation Built Environment

*Foundation mandatory units*
1. Exploring the natural and built environment
2. Exploring buildings, their use and location
3. Investigating working in the built environment

*Foundation optional units*
Three units are required for the full qualification. The list of Built Environment optional units is common to all the awarding bodies, but the choice also extends to the mandatory and optional units of any other Foundation programme.

4.\* Contributing to a team activity
5. Investigating construction craft practices
6. Investigating drawing activities

7.* Health and safety
8. Exploring city communities and new towns
9. The science of buildings

*Core skills units at Level 1*
1. Application of number
2. Communication
3. Information technology

## Intermediate Built Environment

*Intermediate mandatory units*
1. Built environment and the community
2. The science of materials and their applications
3. Construction technology and design
4. Construction operations

*Intermediate optional units*
Two optional units are required for the full qualification. The choice will depend upon the awarding body and what the centre offers where you study.

*Core Skills units at Level 2*
1. Application of number
2. Communication
3. Information Technology

## Advanced Built Environment

*Advanced mandatory units*
1. Built environment and the community
2. Design, detailing and specification
3. The science of materials and their applications
4. Construction and civil engineering technology
5. Construction technology and services
6. Resource management
7. Financing the built environment
8. Surveying processes

*Advanced optional units*
Four optional units are required for the full qualification. The choice will depend upon the awarding body and what the centre offers where you study.

*Core skills units at Level 3*
1. Application of number
2. Communication
3. Information technology

**ENGINEERING**

This GNVQ is a broad-based study of engineering. It will provide you with the learning and skills that underpin the creation of engineered products, engineering systems and services required by modern engineering activity. It also provides opportunities to address wider issues concerned with the value of engineering to society and the environment. For employment, this GNVQ will take you into technician engineering, ie junior draughtsperson, work study officer, problem solving and project engineering. Or you can progress onto an HND or degree course.

You can focus on a specialism through the *optional pathways*, which can be further developed through the *additional units pathways*.

NB. If you are interested in civil and structural engineering, look at the Construction and the Built Environment programme.

## Foundation Engineering

*Foundation mandatory units*
1. Designing engineered products
2. Making engineered products
3. Investigating working in engineering

*Foundation optional units*
Three units are required for the full qualification. The list of Engineering optional units is common to all the awarding bodies, but the choice also extends to the mandatory and optional units of any other Foundation programme.

4. Engineering teamwork
5. Exploring maths and science through engineered products
6. Application of computers in engineering
7. Servicing and repairing engineered products

51

8. Introduction to automation in engineering
9. Health and Safety in engineering

*Core skills units at Level 1*
1. Application of number
2. Communication
3. Information technology

## Intermediate Engineering

*Intermediate mandatory units*
1. Engineering materials and processes
2. Graphical communication in engineering
3. Science and mathematics for engineering
4. Engineering in society and the environment

*Intermediate optional units*
Two optional units are required for the full qualification. The choice will depend upon the awarding body and what the centre offers where you study. There are four pathways of optional units:

   (i)   general
  (ii)   engineering/business
 (iii)   electrical/electronic
 (iv)   motor vehicle

However, if you intend to progress to Advanced Engineering you are *strongly recommended* to select Mathematics (Intermediate) as one of your optional units.

*Core skills units at Level 2*
1. Application of number
2. Communication
3. Information technology

## Advanced Engineering

*Advanced mandatory units*
1. Engineering and commercial functions in business
2. Engineering systems
3. Engineering processes

4. Engineering materials
5. Design development
6. Engineering in society and the environment
7. Science for engineering
8. Mathematics for engineering

*Advanced optional units*
Four optional units are required for the full qualification. The choice will depend upon the awarding body and what the centre offers where you study. There are four pathways of optional units:

(i) general
(ii) mechanical
(iii) electrical/electronic
(iv) motor vehicle

However, if you intend to progress to higher education on completion of this course, you are *strongly recommended* to select Mathematics (Advanced) as one of your optional units.

*Core skills units at Level 3*
1. Application of number
2. Communication
3. Information technology

### HEALTH AND SOCIAL CARE

If you are interested in working in the caring professions, this GNVQ will help you develop your skills and knowledge across a broad range of client groups and types of care provision. The programme will look at all types of care, eg institutional care, care in the community, the social services. And you will learn how to work with all those in need of care. You will also learn about health and development. If you plan to enter nursing, you are strongly advised to select optional units relating to biological science at Advanced level.

## Foundation Health and Social Care

*Foundation mandatory units*
1. Understanding health and well-being
2. Understanding personal development and relationships
3. Investigating working in health and social care

*Foundation optional units*
Three units are required for the full qualification. The list of Health and Social Care optional units is common to all the awarding bodies, but the choice also extends to the mandatory and optional units of any other Foundation programme.

4.* Contributing to a team activity
5. Investigating common health emergencies
6. Planning diets
7.* Exploring health and recreational activities
8. Exploring physical care
9. Investigating health and care service provision

*Core skills units at Level 1*
1. Application of number
2. Communication
3. Information technology

## Intermediate Health and Social Care

*Intermediate mandatory units*
1. Promoting health and well-being
2. Influences on health and well-being
3. Health and social care services
4. Communication and inter-personal relationships in Health and Social Care

*Intermediate optional units*
Two optional units are required for the full qualification. The choice will depend upon the awarding body and what the centre offers where you study.

*Core skills units at Level 2*
1. Application of number
2. Communication
3. Information technology

## Advanced Health and Social Care

*Advanced mandatory units*
1. Equal opportunities and individuals' rights
2. Interpersonal interaction in Health and Social Care
3. Physical aspects of health and social well-being
4. Psycho-social aspects of Health and Social well-being
5. Structure and development of Health and Social Care services
6. Health and social care practice
7. Educating for health and social well-being
8. Research perspectives in Health and Social Care

*Advanced optional units*
Four optional units are required for the full qualification. The choice will depend upon the awarding body and what the centre offers where you study.

*Core skills units at Level 3*
1. Application of number
2. Communication
3. Information technology

### HOSPITALITY AND CATERING

This GNVQ will introduce you to all aspects of the industry from the production and service of food and drink to the providers of accommodation. You will develop skills and knowledge in these areas, along with all aspects of hygiene, purchasing and customer care.

The qualification can be achieved without a work experience element, although work placements are available for many GNVQ students.

# Foundation Hospitality and Catering

*Foundation mandatory units*
1. Exploring food and drink preparation and service
2. Exploring accommodation operations
3. Investigating working in hospitality and catering

*Foundation optional units*
Three units are required for the full qualification. The list of Hospitality and Catering optional units is common to all the awarding bodies, but the choice also extends to the mandatory and optional units of any other Foundation programme.

4.* Contributing to a team activity
5. Investigating front-office operations and accommodation services
6.* Planning diets
7. Health, safety and hygiene in hospitality and catering
8. Purchasing, costing and control in hospitality and catering
9. Providing service to customers in hospitality and catering

*Core skills units at Level 1*
1. Application of number
2. Communication
3. Information technology

# Intermediate Hospitality and Catering

*Intermediate mandatory units*
1. Investigate hospitality and catering
2. Customer service in hospitality and catering
3. Provide front-office and accommodation operations
4. Provide food and drink

*Intermediate optional units*
Two optional units are required for the full qualification. The choice will depend upon the awarding body and what the centre offers where you study.

*Core skills units at Level 2*
1. Application of number
2. Communication
3. Information technology

## Advanced Hospitality and Catering

*Advanced mandatory units*
1. Investigate the hospitality and catering industry
2. Human resources
3. Provide customer service in hospitality and catering
4. Food preparation and cooking
5. Food and drink service
6. Purchasing, costing and finance
7. Accommodation operations
8. Reception and front-office operations in hospitality

*Advanced optional units*
Four optional units are required for the full qualification. The choice will depend upon the awarding body and what the centre offers where you study.

*Core skills units at Level 3*
1. Application of number
2. Communication
3. Information technology

### INFORMATION TECHNOLOGY

This GNVQ is aimed at giving you a good grounding in the use of information technology, whether you are thinking of IT as a career, or where an understanding of the subject will help you study and work more effectively in the future.

## Foundation Information Technology

*Foundation mandatory units*
1. Introduction to Information technology
2. Using Information technology
3. Investigating working in Information technology

**All you need to know about GNVQs**

*Foundation optional units*
Three units are required for the full qualification. The list of Information Technology optional units is common to all the awarding bodies, but the choice also extends to the mandatory and optional units of any other Foundation programme.

4.\* Information technology teamwork
5.  Document production
6.  Graphic design
7.  Modelling and control
8.  Obtaining information from electronic sources
9.  Information collection and processing

*Core skills units at Level 1*
1. Application of number
2. Communication
3. Information technology

## Intermediate Information Technology

*Intermediate mandatory units*
1. Introduction to Information technology
2. Using Information technology
3. Organizations and Information technology
4. Communications and Information technology

*Intermediate optional units*
Two optional units are required for the full qualification. The choice will depend upon the awarding body and what the centre offers where you study.

*Core skills units at Level 2*
1. Application of number
2. Communication
3. Information technology

## Advanced Information Technology

*Advanced mandatory units*
1. Information technology systems
2. Using Information technology
3. Organizations and Information technology
4. Communications and networking
5. Systems analysis
6. Software

7. Database development
8. Information technology projects and teamwork

*Intermediate optional units*
Two optional units are required for the full qualification. The choice will depend upon the awarding body and what the centre offers where you study.

*Core skills units at Level 3*
1. Application of number
2. Communication
3. Information technology

---

### LEISURE AND TOURISM

This GNVQ programme combines leisure and recreation with travel and tourism. It helps you to understand how the two industries attempt to satisfy people's demands and helps you to develop an in-depth knowledge and understanding of the leisure and tourism sector and its component industries. The course includes practical investigation and covers the private, public and voluntary sectors. The Advanced Leisure and Tourism GNVQ will give you the opportunity to specialize in either sport and recreation or travel and tourism through the *optional units pathways*.

## Foundation Leisure and Tourism

*Foundation mandatory units*
1. Providing service to customers
2. Preparing visitor information materials
3. Investigating working in the Leisure and Tourism industries

*Foundation optional units*
Three units are required for the full qualification. The list of Leisure and Tourism optional units is common to all the awarding bodies, but the choice also extends to the mandatory and optional units of any other Foundation programme.

4.* Contributing to a team activity
5. Presentation and display
6. Planning itineraries and making bookings

7. Exploring the provision of travel and tourism products and services
8.* Exploring recreational activities in Leisure and Tourism
9. Processing payments and basic budgeting

*Core skills units at Level 1*
1. Application of number
2. Communication
3. Information technology

## Intermediate Leisure and Tourism

*Intermediate mandatory units*
1. Investigating the leisure and tourism industries
2. Marketing and promoting of leisure and tourism products
3. Customer service in leisure and tourism
4. Contributing to the running of an event

*Intermediate optional units*
Two optional units are required for the full qualification. The choice will depend upon the awarding body and what the centre offers where you study.

*Core skills units at Level 2*
1. Application of number
2. Communication
3. Information technology

## Advanced Leisure and Tourism

*Advanced mandatory units*
1. Investigating the leisure and tourism industries
2. Human resources in the leisure and tourism industries
3. Marketing in leisure and tourism
4. Finance in the leisure and tourism industries
5. Business systems in the leisure and tourism industries
6. Developing customer service in leisure and tourism
7. Health, safety and security in leisure and tourism
8. Event management

*Advanced optional units*
Four optional units are required for the full qualification. The choice will depend upon the awarding body and what the centre offers where you study.

*Core skills units at Level 3*
1. Application of number
2. Communication
3. Information technology

### MANUFACTURING

This GNVQ takes you through all the aspects of manufacturing from product conception to production and marketing. It also looks at the environmental considerations of manufacturing and the role of recycling.

The programme provides a good grounding for further study or the development of expertise in any manufacturing-related specialism.

## Foundation Manufacturing

*Foundation mandatory units*
1. Manufacturing products
2. Exploring manufacturing operations
3. Investigating working in manufacturing

*Foundation optional units*
Three units are required for the full qualification. The list of Manufacturing optional units is common to all the awarding bodies, but the choice also extends to the mandatory and optional units of any other Foundation programme.

4.* Contributing to a team activity
5.* Exploring service to customers
6.* Health and safety in Manufacturing
7. Making a product
8. Investigating the environmental impact of manufacturing operations
9. Maintaining quality of products

*Core skills units at Level 1*
1. Application of number
2. Communication
3. Information technology

## Intermediate manufacturing

*Intermediate mandatory units*
1. The world of Manufacturing
2. Working with a design brief
3. Production planning, costing and quality assurance
4. Manufacturing products

*Intermediate optional units*
Two optional units are required for the full qualification. The choice will depend upon the awarding body and what the centre offers where you study.

*Core skills units at Level 2*
1. Application of number
2. Communication
3. Information technology

## Advanced Manufacturing

*Advanced mandatory units*
1. Manufacturing and the economy
2. Marketing products
3. Work practices
4. Design, development and presentation
5. Production planning, costing and quality assurance
6. Process operations
7. Computer applications in manufacturing
8. Environmental impact

*Advanced optional units*
Four optional units are required for the full qualification. The choice will depend upon the awarding body and what the centre offers where you study.

*Core skills units at Level 3*
1. Application of number
2. Communication
3. Information technology

**SCIENCE**

The Science GNVQ is designed to develop your learning through experiencing the types of activity that scientists carry out, eg experimenting and testing to gather data, analysing things, obtaining substances, developing artefacts, solving problems and maintaining systems. Your study will also address economic, social and environmental issues around the practice of science. Intermediate level could be a useful course for those considering nursing, agriculture or engineering. Study at Advanced level can take you on to a career in science, either through higher levels of study or into science-based employment (eg chemical production, hospital laboratories, or the various forms of engineering).

## Foundation Science

*Foundation mandatory units*
1. Working on scientific tasks
2. Health and safety in science activities
3. Investigating working in science

*Foundation optional units*
Three units are required for the full qualification. The list of Science optional units is common to all the awarding bodies, but the choice also extends to the mandatory and optional units of any other Foundation programme.

4.* Contributing to a team activity
5. Growing, harvesting and processing
6. Repairing and maintaining things
7. Sport, leisure and health
8. Food science
9. Living things and materials in the environment

*Core skills units at Level 1*
1. Application of number
2. Communication
3. Information technology

**All you need to know about GNVQs**

## Intermediate Science

*Intermediate mandatory units*
1. Work on scientific tasks
2. Investigate living things, materials and substances
3. Make useful products
4. Monitor and control systems

*Intermediate optional units*
Two optional units are required for the full qualification. The choice will depend upon the awarding body and what the centre offers where you study.

*Core skills units at Level 2*
1. Application of number
2. Communication
3. Information technology

## Advanced Science

*Advanced mandatory units*
1. Laboratory safety and analysis of samples
2. Investigate materials and their use
3. Obtain new substances
4. Obtain products from organisms
5. Control the transfer of energy
6. Control reactions
7. Human physiology and healthcare management
8. Communicating information

*Advanced optional units*
Four optional units are required for the full qualification. The choice will depend upon the awarding body and what the centre offers where you study.

*Core skills units at Level 3*
1. Application of number
2. Communication
3. Information technology

# PILOT GNVQs

Three new GNVQ programme areas are being introduced and piloted at selected centres from September 1995. These are:

- Management Studies (Advanced level only)
- Media: Communication and Production (Intermediate and Advanced levels only)
- Retail & Distributive Services (Intermediate and Advanced levels only)

### MANAGEMENT STUDIES

The Management Studies GNVQ is only available at Advanced level and is still being piloted in selected centres in 1995/96
This GNVQ is intended for those interested in becoming managers (preferably with at least some work experience but with little or no managerial experience).
It provides a path for those wishing to progress through education to further management qualifications, or into a variety of other employment opportunities. It is also an alternative for those who are unable to have access to an NVQ in Management through lack of appropriate work responsibilities.

## Advanced Management Studies

*Advanced mandatory units*
1. Manager's responsibilities
2. Organizations and Managers' roles
3. Services and products
4. Customer relationships
5. Interpersonal communication
6. Employment, recruitment and development
7. Budgets and accounts
8. Handling information

*Advanced optional units*
Four optional units are required for the full qualification. The choice

will depend upon the awarding body and what the centre offers where you study.

*Core skills units at Level 3*
1. Application of number
2. Communication
3. Information technology

### MEDIA: COMMUNICATION AND PRODUCTION

On this GNVQ, which is available at Intermediate and Advanced levels only, you will produce media items and finished media products in line with professional practice. Not only will you learn how to handle and use equipment and materials, but you will also develop an understanding of the relevant theory.

## Intermediate Media: Communication and Production

*Intermediate mandatory units*
1. Investigating media products and audiences
2. Planning and producing a print and graphic product
3. Planning and producing an audio-visual product
4. Investigating local, regional and national media

*Intermediate optional units*
Two optional units are required for the full qualification. The choice will depend upon the awarding body and what the centre offers where you study.

*Core skills units at Level 2*
1. Application of number
2. Communication
3. Information technology

## Advanced Media: Communication and Production

*Advanced mandatory units*
1. Investigating the content of media products
2. Originating and producing print and graphics material
3. Planning and producing print and graphics products

4. Planning audio-visual production
5. Producing audio-visual products
6. Investigating and carrying out media research
7. Investigating and carrying out media marketing
8. Investigating media industries in the UK and abroad

*Advanced optional units*

Four optional units are required for the full qualification. The choice will depend upon the awarding body and what the centre offers where you study.

*Core skills units at Level 3*

1. Application of number
2. Communication
3. Information technology

### RETAIL & DISTRIBUTIVE SERVICES

This GNVQ, which is available at Intermediate and Advancad levels only, will give you a head start into a dynamic and fast-growing area which employs five million men and women. You will learn about and experience the many aspects of this exciting environment including retail, marketing, management, transport, international trade, warehousing and stock control, and finance.

The course will prepare you as a trainee manager, or equip you to progress to higher education.

## Intermediate Retail & Distributive Services

*Intermediate mandatory units*

1. Distribution, transport and storage
2. Quality and service to the customer
3. Retailing and sales
4. Administration and finance

*Intermediate optional units*

Two optional units are required for the full qualification. The choice will depend upon the awarding body and what the centre offers where you study.

**All you need to know about GNVQs**

*Core skills units at Level 2*
1. Application of number
2. Communication
3. Information technology

## Advanced Retail & Distributive Services

*Advanced mandatory units*
1. Transport and storage
2. Quality and customer service
3. Marketing and sales
4. Purchasing and stock control
5. Finance and administration
6. Responsibilities of managers
7. Human resourcing
8. International trade and distribution

*Advanced optional units*
Four optional units are required for the full qualification. The choice will depend upon the awarding body and what the centre offers where you study.

*Core skills units at Level 3*
1. Application of number
2. Communication
3. Information technology

# Pilot courses for September 1996

Two further GNVQ programmes to be piloted in selected centres in September 1996 are:

■ Landbased & Environmental Industries
■ Performing Arts.

# 4

# Core Skills

*'The core skills of communication, application of number, and information technology, coupled with personal skills give young people the practical experience they need to succeed at work, and particularly in retailing. That is why we are happy to launch the GNVQ Scholarship scheme at Sainsbury's this year (1995).'*

Andrew Tanner, Corporate Resourcing, J Sainsbury plc

---

**CHAPTER SUMMARY**

This chapter explains:

▶ what the core skills are
▶ how they form part of a GNVQ.

---

'Core skills' is the term used in GNVQ to describe skills that are essential in both our private and working life: skills that we need for dealing with people; being able to understand when we are presented with numbers; and knowing how to use a computer.

On a GNVQ programme, the skills of language and communication, number, and information technology are not taught in isolation. You learn how to apply these skills in different situations.

Q~ Think of an occasion such as applying for a GNVQ course or applying for a job. Can you list all the skills required which would give you the best possible chance of success? (Check with the model answer below.)

We often take for granted the skills we already use. On the course, you will develop these skills and become more effective at using them. Every time you carry out a piece of work – a project, an assignment, or an activity – the core skills will be identified and your achievement will be recorded. Your work will be the evidence that you have achieved the outcomes required by the core skills.

A~ You need to do some planning and preparation, including research; write (and possibly word-process) an application using a good style of English, without spelling mistakes, and appropriately laid out; you must describe yourself and your achievements in a way that puts you in the best possible light; and then at the interview you will have to present yourself and communicate with a stranger whilst appearing confident, competent and at ease!

This is what the core skills are all about.

# THE CORE SKILLS

The three core skills which are mandatory on every GNVQ programme are:

- Communication
- Application of number
- Information technology.

Three more core skills units are available:

- Personal skills – working with others
- Personal skills – improving own learning and performance
- Problem solving.

The units in personal skills are recommended and can be taken as additional units. The problem solving unit has not yet been accredited.
  Core skills are the same for GNVQs and NVQs. As there are five levels for NVQs, core skills units have been developed for levels 1 to 5. Each level includes everything described at the previous level, so if you achieve core skills at level 3 you are competent at levels 1 and 2.

Core skills levels are designed to correspond with the National Curriculum as follows:

| Core skills unit level | National Curriculum level |
|:---:|:---:|
| 1 | 4 and below |
| 2 | 5 and 6 |
| 3 | 7 |
| 4 | 8 and 9 |
| 5 | 10 and above |

# STRUCTURE

Just as with GNVQ vocational units, the core skills are statements of outcomes and the structure of a core skills unit is the same as a GNVQ vocational unit:

- *elements* describe the activity to be assessed
- *performance criteria* provide a means of judging successful performance
- *range statements* describe the range of settings in which the activity should be performed successfully
- *evidence indicators* are the work to be produced for assessment.

(For a more detailed explanation, see Chapter 2.)

# CONTENT

Whatever the GNVQ programme, you must take the core skills units of Communication, Application of number, and Information technology written for the level of the course you are doing. For instance, if you are taking an Intermediate GNVQ then you will take core skills for level 2. However, if your skills reflect the standard for a higher level, then you can be credited with the higher level core skills units.

## Communication

The communication skills developed here are interpreting language, and using language to present information and ideas. You will use these skills in speaking, listening, writing and reading. The units in

Communication identify four key themes:

1. taking part in discussions
2. producing written materials
3. using images to illustrate points made in writing and discussions
4. reading and responding to written materials and images.

Each level requires a more sophisticated use of communication skills than the level below, and the situations in which you practise these skills will be more demanding.

For example, at level 2, you will take part in a discussion on something straightforward with someone you may or may not know, but who will be familiar with the subject. Your contribution to the discussion should take the discussion forward. At level 3, the topic for discussion will be more complex and with someone who doesn't know anything about it. During the discussion you must create the opportunity for others to contribute.

|  | **Level 2** | **Level 3** |
|---|---|---|
| subject of discussion | straightforward | straightforward and complex |
| with a person who is... | known or unknown | known or unknown |
| that person is... | familiar with subject | familiar and not familiar with subject |
| student required to... | take discussion forward | take discussion forward and create opportunities for others to contribute |

**Table 4.1** Communication: taking part in discussions

(You will notice, as pointed out above, how each level includes the requirements of the previous level.)

# Application of number

As the title suggests, these units ask you to show how numbers are applied in any given situation. For example, it is not knowing how to calculate a percentage, but being able to use percentages to solve a problem. Each level will demand more complex techniques to be used.

The units in Application of number identify three key themes:

1. gathering and processing data
2. representing and tackling problems
3. interpreting and presenting data.

## Information technology

These units describe how information technology is to be used in completing practical tasks. The stages of development reflected in the levels demand broader knowledge in the use of information technology and more complex operations to be performed. The units in Information technology identify five key themes:

1. entering and storing information
2. editing and organizing information
3. presenting information
4. evaluating procedures and features of applications
5. dealing with errors and faults.

# HOW CORE SKILLS ARE INTEGRATED

You show your ability in core skills by the way you handle the work required for the vocational units.

If we take Unit 1: 'Business in the economy', from Advanced Business then Unit 3: 'Health and social care services', from Intermediate Health and Social Care, we can see how vocational units can involve core skills.

## Advanced Business

### Unit 1: Business in the economy

Element 1.1     Analyse the forces of supply and demand on businesses

Element 1.2     Analyse the operation of markets and their effects on businesses and communities

Element 1.3     Examine the effects of government policies on markets

The work carried out to cover these elements in Unit 1 could demonstrate core skills as follows.

*The Communication skills at level 3 could include:*

3.1 discuss economics with level 2 students
3.2 produce written material
3.3 produce bar charts, pie charts, maps, diagrams and photographs
3.4 read newspaper articles, textbooks and economic resource materials and list sources of information

*The Application of number skills at level 3 could include:*

3.1        collect information for a portfolio of shares, design a questionnaire on privatization and analyse results

3.2 and 3.3    from the portfolio of shares, represent each share as a proportion of whole; produce a spreadsheet and calculate cost of each share, proceeds of sale and profit, and interpret data

*Information technology skills at level 3 could include:*

       using a computer for word-processing reports and questionnaires;
       spreadsheets, preparation of graphs and tables and data analysis

# Intermediate Health & Social Care

A student on Intermediate Health & Social Care undertook a project on 'Meeting people's needs' for Unit 3 'Health and social care services'. Part of the project included identifying the structure of health and care services, which required an explanation of the relationship between key services, central Government and local provision. As these services overlap, the student chose to illustrate this in her written work by using a Venn diagram as shown in Figure 4.1. This use of this diagram satisfied Communication core skill, Element 2.3: the use of images to illustrate points made in writing.

The whole project was carried out over three terms. At the end, our student took part in a group presentation to inform other students in her year of the health and care services available. Her final portfolio of work for the project included lists, written summaries, an essay, a questionnaire, a case study, charts and diagrams, and work experience at a residential home for older people. She met the requirements to pass seven elements in Communication and Information Technology core skills.

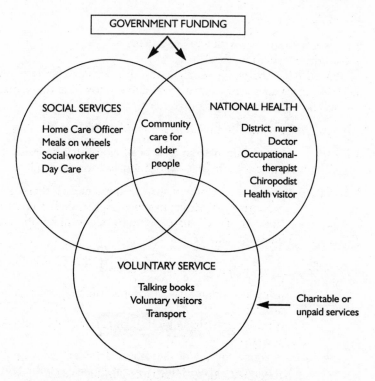

**Figure 4.1** Services working together for older people

For this project, the students were given a very general brief and were expected to structure a complex activity themselves. This meant the project could provide evidence for a distinction grade.

# 5

# Alternatives to GNVQ

By 1997, the Government wants to see 80% of young people achieving four GCSEs or their equivalent. And by the year 2000, 60% achieving two A levels or their equivalent.

---

**CHAPTER SUMMARY**

The national framework of qualifications provides you with the choice of academic and vocational qualifications – with NVQs available from level 1 up to level 4 or 5. This chapter explains academic and vocational qualifications which would be alternatives to GNVQs at levels 1 to 3, and includes:

▶ GCSEs
▶ GCE A and AS levels
▶ job-specific vocational courses
▶ NVQs
▶ C&G Technological Baccalaureate
▶ Baccalaureate
▶ combination of GCE A, AS, and GNVQ.

---

## LEVEL 1

City & Guilds offers a Diploma in Vocational Education. This is a one-year course and will introduce you to the world of work through projects and work experience. There are several work areas which include Art, Business Studies, Services to People, and Technical Services. However 1995/96 may be the last year this is offered.

There are other vocational choices at this level, including NVQs, but consult your school or local college.

# LEVEL 2

## GCSEs

GCSEs are firmly established and widely recognized. GCSEs will take you onto a GNVQ Advanced. If you are considering going on to higher education, and for some employment, you will be in a stronger position and have a wider choice if you have GCSE maths and English. Many universities will stipulate GCSE maths and English in addition to GNVQ Advanced. Some universities are beginning to recognize Intermediate GNVQ as an alternative to four or five GCSEs. GCSEs are available in vocational areas, for example, Business Studies, Information Technology, Design and Technology with Art or Electronics or Fashion.

## Vocational

Examining boards such as RSA and City & Guilds offer hundreds of single-subject examinations as well as group examinations in an extensive range of job areas. You will learn the skills and knowledge directly related to types of work. Many of the vocational areas are available as NVQs, and may be offered by your local school or college as well as by employers.

# LEVEL 3

Studies at level 3 are a quantum leap from level 2. You will find GCE A and AS levels on the academic side, although some schools may offer S (special or scholarship) level papers.

But whether GCE or GNVQ, you will find the work is tougher and will require greater application and self-discipline. There will be new vocabularies and concepts to grapple with, and you will need to produce work based on your own research and reading.

# GCE A levels

A levels are taken as single subjects, and studied in depth. Some include assessment based on coursework as well as a final exam, while others are exam only. They are usually two-year courses, and will have an exam at the end of the first year which requires a pass to progress to the second year. A few A levels are now modular with an exam at the end of each module.

Studying for A levels is very different from the requirements of GNVQs. You will be required to write essays, working mostly on your own. The qualifying exam, with each paper of perhaps two to three hours duration, is sat at the end of the course. A university place offer will be based on your 'predicted' grades.

Certainly A levels have a kudos which attracts students. For some career paths, A levels are a must, ie medicine and dentistry. And an A level does allow a student to study in depth a single subject in which they are particularly interested or able. However, for an A level programme there is evidence to suggest that students with fewer than five GCSE passes at grade C or above do not fare well. I think it is only fair here to mention some of the weaknesses in the A level provision. By definition it is a narrow and not a comprehensive level of study. Many GCE A level programmes consist of no more than a two or three subject curriculum with little regard paid to the relationship of one subject to another. It does not prepare people for work and may neglect the development of core skills, particularly in information technology, as well as communication and numerical ability. Those students who choose an A level course and then regret it and drop out, or who fail their final exams, rarely obtain recognition for partial achievement.

Universities do like A levels as entry to degree courses, but you will be required to meet minimum grades in usually three subjects. If you don't achieve the grades you need, you will have to wait to resit the exam or re-do some or all of the course.

The following table gives a breakdown of the number of students who sat A level examinations in 1992–93, and the percentage pass rate of those students. The final column shows what percentage of the students gained A–C grades.

| | Number of entrants | Percentage pass A–E | Percentage pass A–C |
|---|---|---|---|
| *Schools* | | | |
| 18 year olds | 364,000 | 83 | 52 |
| 19 year olds and over | 52,000 | 72 | 38 |
| *Sixth form colleges* | | | |
| 18 year olds | 79,000 | 83 | 50 |
| 19 year olds and over | 23,000 | 73 | 35 |
| *Tertiary colleges* | | | |
| 18 year olds | 32,000 | 79 | 45 |
| 19 year olds and over | 27,000 | 65 | 32 |
| *Other FE colleges* | | | |
| 18 year olds | 30,000 | 70 | 36 |
| 19 year olds and over | 95,000 | 62 | 31 |
| TOTALS | 702,000 | 78 | 45 |

**Table 5.1** GCE A level examination results (England) 1992–93
Source: Department for Education and Employment

GNVQs are broader-based qualifications assessed on practical work which will also show your knowledge of theory. Some centres will set timed assignments under exam conditions for some modules, for example Finance. The external tests for GNVQ units have to be sat under exam conditions, and these are based on multiple-choice questions which cover the whole syllabus, and last for one hour. However, there are three times during the year when these tests can be sat, so they can be taken soon after completion of a unit.

# AS

AS, or 'advanced supplementary', are half an A level, so two AS levels are equal to one A level. They are a good way of broadening an A level programme, for example, taking two A levels and one or two AS levels. An A level programme would not normally be made up of AS levels only. AS levels can also enhance an Advanced GNVQ.

## Vocational

There are hundreds of vocational courses to cover highly specific fields of work (so by definition cannot be GNVQs but may be NVQs). Some have a progression structure which lead to levels 3 and 4, others may be suitable as entry qualifications to higher level courses including vocational HNDs (higher national diplomas) and degrees.

Some will be recognized towards membership and qualifications of professional bodies. For example, BTEC National in Environmental Health Studies leads to a related degree course, and is also recognized by the Institution of Environmental Health Officers for entry to its Diploma in Environmental Health, with professional qualification on completion. C&G Media Techniques in Print & Radio Journalism or Television & Video, is a good preparation for the National Council for Training of Journalists awards.

These courses can cover a wide range, including: agriculture, beauty therapy, child care, engineering, fibre optics, floristry, forestry, funeral services, home economics, horticulture, interior design, marine technology, mining, motor vehicle studies, pet store management, photography, radio amateurs, plus courses in the various fields of science, technology, design, graphics and printing.

In 1995 BTEC announced that, while there is demand, it would be continuing the BTEC National courses which were to be discontinued in preference to GNVQs. So there now exists a choice, for example, between a BTEC National in Business or a BTEC Advanced GNVQ in Business – although both are unlikely to be available in the same subject within one school or college.

# NVQs (NATIONAL VOCATIONAL QUALIFICATIONS)

You can continue to gain qualifications when you are at work either by taking part-time or evening study or through acquiring NVQs in the workplace. NVQs are competence-based and relate to the work you are doing. They cover a range of specific occupations (see also 'Vocational' above) and are available from level 1 up to level 4 or 5. When you are job-hunting, find out what employers offer. Alternatively you can find out more information direct from the Awarding Bodies, and you can obtain a full list of these from NCVQ.

# C&G TECHNOLOGICAL BACCALAUREATE (ADVANCED)

The TechBac is a level 3 qualification. It has been designed to bridge academic and vocational routes and encourage a breadth of studies. It is seen as an enhancement to A levels and GNVQ by giving a further qualification, but it can also be an alternative to a full GNVQ, by offering technological studies together with the study of A levels. It was introduced in 1991 by City & Guilds and piloted for three years. It is generally available from September 1995.

A student is able to achieve a TechBac (Advanced) with a minimum of two A levels (or an equivalent combination of AS examinations), or a GNVQ at advanced level plus the Technological Studies component.

It has a component structure of four study areas: specialist studies, technological studies, broadening studies, and management of learning. Table 5.2 illustrates this.

| Technological Studies | Broadening Studies | | Specialist Studies |
|---|---|---|---|
| Designing and Making or Managing Practical Action | Maths | Science | A/AS examinations |
| plus Understanding Technological Change | Creative Studies | Foreign Language | or GNVQ |
| Management of Learning | | | |

**Table 5.2** Components of study of the TechBac

The following tables are examples of a possible programme of study for an A level science student, and a Leisure & Tourism GNVQ Advanced student.

Example 1: A student taking science A levels and interested in becoming a chemical engineer

| Technological Studies | Broadening Studies | | Specialist Studies |
|---|---|---|---|
| Projects:<br>1. Designing a simple chemical production system | MEI Mathematics unit | Science credit unit transfer from Specialist studies | A levels in Chemistry Physics |
| 2. Understanding technological change within the chemical industry | C&G Photography modules | C&G Vocational Language units | |
| Management of Learning | | | |

**Table 5.3** Example of the TechBach for a science A level student

Example 2: A student taking Advanced GNVQ in Leisure & Tourism and interested in leisure centre management

| Technological Studies | Broadening Studies | | Specialist Studies |
|---|---|---|---|
| Projects:<br>1. Designing a management information system | Application of Number credit transfer from Specialist Studies | Modular A level unit in Mechanics [forces] | GNVQ [Advanced] in Leisure & Tourism |
| 2. Understanding technological change within the teaching of languages | GNVQ Media unit | Foreign Languiage credit transfer from Specialist Studies | with Foreign Language optional units |
| Management of Learning | | | |

**Table 5.4** Example of the TechBac for a Leisure & Tourism GNVQ Advanced student

# COMBINATION OF GCE A, AS AND GNVQ

It is possible to combine A levels with GNVQs. For A level students, the addition of GNVQ units will enhance and extend studies. This may be subject-related, for example, in Art and Design a GNVQ unit could give you more hands-on experience in jewellery or model making; or profession-related, eg adding a GNVQ module in professional studies for teaching; or extending your skills with a GNVQ unit in information technology. If you are following a GNVQ programme, you may need an A or AS level in a related subject. You will need to find out from the centre where you study what opportunities exist to combine vocational and academic studies.

*A word of advice.* Do bear in mind that your priority is to do well and to get the best grades you can. So don't take on any extra work unless you are absolutely sure you will still get the grades you need, and that you will be able to adjust to the different styles of teaching and assessment. Talk over your career plans with your careers officer and tutor and put together a timetable of study which is best suited to you.

# BACCALAUREATE

Another choice at 16 is the not-so-common Baccalaureate. This is another broad-based qualification and has academic and vocational pathways: the International Baccalaureate and the Technological Baccalaureate.

If you are thinking of working or studying abroad, the GNVQ – as a new qualification in this country – may not be as readily recognized as A levels and the Baccalaureate. (See also 'European degrees' in Chapter 8.)

# SUMMARY

A levels are single subjects, studied in depth and academic. There is little or no cross-fertilization between subjects, they do not develop core skills and do not prepare you for work. However, they are the most well-established and widely-known advanced level qualification. Universities use A levels as the benchmark for entry. GNVQs (or vocational A levels) are modular, broadly based and practical. They are not so well established as A levels. In some quarters there is some criticism of them, but they are designed to be at the same standard as A levels and have parity of esteem. GNVQ Advanced leads to a related degree.

At level 3, essentially your choice will be directed by how you learn best as well as what you want to study. I have known students who have opted for vocational qualifications because they feared the demands and the examinations of A levels. This is valid, and each student should understand the course conditions that suit them best. However, GNVQs are not a soft option; they are another way of achieving at level 3. The GNVQ programme has a number of different components, all of which must be passed. It is demanding, and you have to put in a lot of work to keep up. If all the mandatory units are taught in the first year, on an advanced level course you may find you have to produce 16 assignments, each to a given deadline, and sit seven external tests. But you are not always working on your own like in A level study. You will work collaboratively in groups, and GNVQ students are usually very supportive of each other. A university place offer will depend on the grades you achieve for your first year's work. However, if you don't manage to pass a unit or external test you will be 'referred' and given the opportunity to try again during the course.

# 6
# Vocational Qualifications in Scotland

CHAPTER SUMMARY

This chapter gives:

► a brief outline of vocational qualifications available in Scotland
► the levels and vocational areas of GSVQs.

Education in Scotland is treated differently from the rest of the UK, and is the responsibility of the Scottish Office Education Department.

## THE VOCATIONAL QUALIFICATIONS FRAMEWORK IN SCOTLAND

Scotland has designed a vocational education system based on individual units of study. Units fall into three categories: National Certificate Modules, Higher National Units and Workplace Assessed Units. Together they provide the opportunity for vocational study from the age of 14 (linked to the school curriculum) to postgraduate/post-experience level.

Each vocational unit covers a particular topic area. Units can be studied individually or put together to form group awards such as the following:

## All you need to know about GNVQs

- National Certificate Awards (which includes GSVQs)
- SVQs
- Higher National Certificates and Higher National Diplomas
- Professional Development Awards.

The Scottish vocational educational framework is as follows

| Description | Group Awards | |
|---|---|---|
| | SVQs | GSVQs and HNC/HND |
| Professional | Level V | Higher National Diplomas |
| Higher Technician/ Junior Management | Level IV | Higher National Certificates |
| Technician, Advanced Craft, Supervisor | Level III | GSVQ National Certificate Group Award Level III |
| Basic Craft | Level II | GSVQ National Certificate Group Award Level II |
| Foundation | Level I | GSVQ National Certificate Group Award Level II |
| For those who have been out of paid employment for some time and need to rebuild their confidence, or have no formal qualifications | National Certificate Skillstart 2 | |
| For slow learners, including those with mild to moderate learning difficulties | National Certificate Skillstart 1 | |
| Linked to the Scottish School Curriculum. Available to school students from the age of 14. Lifestart is aimed at slower learners and those with mild to moderate learning difficulties | National Certificate Lifestart | Skillstart Suite of awards |
| Linked to the Scottish School Curriculum. Available to school students from the age of 14. Workstart is aimed at slower learners and those with mild to moderate learning difficulties | National Certificate Workstart | |

**Table 6.1** The Scottish framework of vocational qualifications
NB. The equivalences shown are only approximate

# WHAT IS A GSVQ?

A GSVQ is the General Scottish Vocational Qualification and is the equivalent of a GNVQ. GSVQs were introduced in 1992 to provide a stepping-stone to a wide range of employment opportunities as well as to higher education or further training. They are specially designed to meet the needs of 16–19 year olds in school or in further education, and for adults who want to return to study in preparation for employment. They teach the skills and knowledge for an occupational area, such as business administration, design or science.

GSVQs are one part of the Scottish vocational qualifications framework. A GSVQ is made up of National Certificate modules. GSVQs are available at three levels – GSVQ National Certificate Level I, II and III.

Level I is different from the other two levels in that it does not focus on a particular vocational area. It provides a general introduction, and is best suited to those who want more information before choosing a vocational area, or who are not able to meet the qualification requirements for Level II. Level II is currently available in 12 occupational areas, and Level III in 13 areas.

LEVEL I

| GSVQ NATIONAL CERTIFICATE |
| --- |
| A broadly based flexible qualification combining 12 module credits |

LEVEL II

| GSVQ NATIONAL CERTIFICATE | | | | |
| --- | --- | --- | --- | --- |
| Business Admin | Hospitality | Leisure & Tourism | Technology | Care |
| Arts and Social Sciences | Design | Information Technology | Land-based Industries | Science |
| | Construction* | Engineering* | | |
| Each occupational area comprises 13 module credits | | | | |

87

LEVEL III

| GSVQ NATIONAL CERTIFICATE | | | | |
|---|---|---|---|---|
| Business Admin | Hospitality | Leisure & Tourism | Technology | Care |
| Arts and Social Sciences | Design | Information Technology | Land-based Industries | Science |
| | Construction* | Engineering* | Communication and Media | |
| Each occupational area comprises 20 module credits | | | | |

**Table 6.2** GSVQ National Certificate Levels I, II and III
*available from the end of 1996

The total number of units required at each level, ie 20 modules at level III, will be made up of mandatory and optional units, and mandatory core skills units.

# GSVQs – BROAD-BASED AND FLEXIBLE

## A modular programme

GSVQ is a broadly-based vocational qualification. The courses are modular – that is they are made up of units of study from the National Certificate Modules. The total number of modules is made up of *mandatory* modules plus others that you choose (the *optional* modules), and the mandatory *core skills* modules. Each module has a credit value, and a set number of credits (depending on the level) must be passed to receive the full group award.

The flexibility of the modular approach means that it is perfectly possible for a qualification to be obtained through different modes of study, ie full-time, part-time, evening study, day release or block release from employment, or through open learning.

## Certification

As you achieve each unit, it is listed on your personal *Record of Education and Training* (RET). When you have achieved all the units needed for a GSVQ this is recorded on your RET and you will receive a special *GSVQ certificate*. This means you can build up a qualification over time. So if you are not able to follow the full course of study in one go, or if your study is interrupted, you will not have lost the units you have passed.

## Additional Assessment

To achieve the full award at levels II and III, a special project must be undertaken which is known as the *additional assessment*. The project will require you to tackle a real or hypothetical problem or create a complex artefact relevant to your course of study. Your performance on the project will determine whether you receive a *pass or merit grade*.

## Grades

At levels II and III, group awards are graded either Pass or Merit. A Merit grade indicates significant achievement on the course. Individual units are not graded. Your overall grade will be determined by the work submitted for the additional assessment project.

# OTHER NATIONAL CERTIFICATE AWARDS

## National Certificate Cluster

National Certificate Clusters are made up of three units from a single vocational area such as European studies, home economics, or information technology. National Certificate Clusters may be of particular interest to school students. They give a 'taster' of a vocational area.

## Skillstart awards

### Skillstart 1 and Skillstart 2

If you need a less demanding course (which will give you a qualification), either because you have not been involved in mainstream education or you first need to acquire some basic skills, you can now choose one of two Skillstart courses.

### Lifestart and Workstart

These two courses have been designed specifically to fit in with the Scottish school curriculum at S3, ie from the age of 14. They are designed for slower learners and those with mild to moderate learning difficulties.

# SVQs

SVQs are the Scottish equivalent of NVQs. They are designed to meet the needs of particular jobs, and are based on standards set by industry. They are known as an 'occupational' SVQ and are most suited to people who are already in employment. They are available at five levels and are made up of units especially designed to be assessed in the workplace or workplace conditions.

# HNCs AND HNDs

Higher National Certificates and Higher National Diplomas are higher levels of study for a vocational qualification, and are made up of Higher National Units. They may contribute towards the requirements for membership of professional and technical bodies, and may give you entry to the first or second year of a degree course.

# PROFESSIONAL DEVELOPMENT AWARDS

These awards are for people at postgraduate or post-experience level who wish to further develop their career or make a career change. PDAs can be made up of either National Certificate Modules, Higher National Units or Workplace Assessed Units. PDAs are currently available within certain occupations such as engineering, quality assurance, management, business counselling, systems analysis and design, materials management, and Gaelic broadcasting.

# THE SCOTTISH VOCATIONAL EDUCATION COUNCIL (SCOTVEC)

The Scottish Vocational Education Council was established in 1985 by the Secretary of State for Scotland, by merging SCOTEC and SCOTBEC.

SCOTVEC is responsible for developing a comprehensive system of vocational qualifications available as parallel qualifications to the traditional school subjects and will complement Standard grades and

Highers. Unlike the rest of the UK, SCOTVEC is the sole awarding and accrediting body for all Scottish vocational qualifications.

For further information, contact:

SCOTVEC
Hanover House
24 Douglas Street
Glasgow
G2 7NQ
General enquiries tel: 0141–248 7900
Publications Unit tel: 0141–242 2168

# 7

# How to Succeed

*'My advice to anyone doing a GNVQ would be to keep up
with the assignments. Missing deadlines can be bad for
your health!'*

Jessica

---

### CHAPTER SUMMARY

This chapter contains tips and information to help you to get the
most from a GNVQ course:

▶ choosing the right course and establishment
▶ how to present yourself at the interview
▶ tips on being organized
▶ study techniques.

---

## GETTING ONTO THE COURSE

### Which course is for you?

Before you apply for any course of study, you should:

- think where you want to be and what you want to have achieved
  in, say, five years time, so that what you do next fits into that plan
- think carefully about the next course of study and the options open
  to you, discussing this with parents/guardians, teaching staff and
  careers staff
- research into the content and scope of the courses available to you

- study the prospectus and course literature published by centres offering the course or courses which interest you
- and, if you possibly can, speak to students who are on, or who have recently completed those courses – especially at the centre where you want to take the course.

It is also a good idea to find out about the resources and facilities which are available to students at the centre, eg computers, media resources, library facilities, canteen, common room; plus activities, groups, etc organized for students. And what is the centre's general approach to its students?

When you have applied for the course of your choice, you will very likely be asked to attend an interview. How you present at interview will decide whether you are accepted onto the course.

## The Interview

In preparation for the interview, try to achieve the following:

- in advance, read through the centre's published information so that you refresh your memory on what that centre offers
- know why you want to do the course so that at interview you will be able to explain this, pointing out the relevance to you of the course curriculum and how it fits in with your career plans
- be knowledgeable about the course so that you can demonstrate you understand the content and requirements of the course and that you are committed to succeed
- have questions ready and ask these at the end of the interview if they have not been covered during the interview.

# BUILD IN SUCCESS

## Getting off to a good start

To be successful on a GNVQ course, the message from me to you is:

### BE ORGANIZED

And that means right from the beginning. Being organized makes a big difference, not just in keeping up with the course but also for revision and being successful. Being organized will reduce the pressure. There is a saying: 'few people plan to fail, but many fail to plan'.

If you are going on to university, then you will be applying during the first term of your second year. An offer of a university place depends on your first year grades! Which means you are being judged on what you achieve in your first year. Universities will often ask for distinctions. You will want to do as well as you can during that year, so make sure you get off to a good start.

## Organizing your papers

First of all, get a file – preferably a ring-binder – for each module you will be studying. If you are on an Advanced level course, you will probably only need to organize a year at a time. In each binder you will keep everything relating to that unit: eg notes, handouts, research materials, press cuttings, photocopies of articles and texts that relate to the module, and completed assignments. Keeping your work in this way will mean you can readily refer to information when doing assignments, will help you develop and demonstrate your organizational and record-keeping skills – which are an essential part of the course – and will also be an important aid when revising for the external tests.

It is important that you keep lecture notes and assignments in date order, with clear headings.

Also, keep a notebook which you can carry with you to jot down information, ie book titles, articles, new words and expressions – their use, meaning and spelling – programmes to watch or listen, or any other information or ideas you want to remember or do.

Course verifiers and moderators will look at your files as well as your Portfolio of Evidence.

## Equipment

Make sure at the start of the course you have the equipment you will need. The centre will advise or suggest what dictionaries and calculators. They may also offer a reading list. Some centres will have a shop selling your basic equipment needs.

## Managing your time (or 'time management' or 'critical path analysis')

At all levels of sudy it is important to allocate time for study and homework. But studying at level 3 is a quantum leap from level 2. Suddenly you are asked to be an independent learner. You will have a lot more work to do and you will have to find out information for yourself. There are techniques to help you. Treat your course as a project which has to be completed to a deadline.

Think of a project like building a stadium for the Olympic Games: the foundations have to be laid, walls built, services to be laid on like electricity, water and gas. Some of these things can only be done after other work has finished. Some work can be done at the same time. In the same way, so that all the work fits together at the right time and in time for assignment deadlines and tests, you need to manage your time.

Time management is just what you need to ensure you can fit in research, private study, homework and assignments with your lectures and get it all done to a deadline – and have time for a life outside school or college! (Failing to meet a deadline may downgrade your work.)

## YOU ONLY HAVE ONE LIFE!

Draw up timetables: for the year, for each month or term, and for each week. You only have one life and you must organize the competing demands on your time.

Produce a *year plan*: note which modules are being taught, and when the external exams are. Show revision weeks and put in holidays. Add assignment information: when they will be given, the assignment period and the deadline for each assignment. Include work experience (if any). Don't forget to complete the calendar with known commitments from your private life. Now you have an overall picture of the year. Below is an example of a layout you can use, although the first column would be wider for you to enter the information. Week beginning Monday 16 October is shaded to indicate half-term.

The *monthly/termly timetable* will be similar, but daily not weekly. It will include information from the annual timetable, but will show a more detailed breakdown of what you will be doing during this period, ie tasks, appointments, etc, and deadlines to be met.

Your *weekly timetable* will show your waking hours for each day. You will need to fill in the time you will be in school or college: include private study time, workshop/library time and any planned visits. Then how you plan to allocate the rest of your time between college work and your private life.

| Week beginning | Sept | | | Oct | | | | | Nov | | | |
|---|---|---|---|---|---|---|---|---|---|---|---|---|
| | 11 | 18 | 25 | 2 | 9 | 16 | 23 | 30 | 6 | 13 | 20 | 27 |
| Assignment 1 | | | | ← | | → | | | | | | |
| Presentation | | | | | | | ↔ | | | | | |
| Assignment 2 | | | | | | | | | | ← | → | |
| Unit test | | | | | | | | | | | | |
| Xmas holiday | | | | | | | | | | | | |

**Figure 7.1** Example of a yearly planner

## Know the curriculum

A GNVQ programme embraces current thinking and practice. I always advise students to make sure they know the areas of study. By doing this you will pick up on information which will help you with your studies.

Relevant information will be found in books, articles and programmes. So check what is available in the library (centre library or public library); read relevant newspapers, magazines, trade papers and journals; and look out for radio and television programmes, including the news. These sources will help you relate current information and events to the units you are studying, and may even provide you with some good quotes!

## Study skills

There are some very important study skills which you really should spend time on developing. Mastery of these skills will improve your ability to learn and improve your performance in assignment work. I am listing some of these skills because students do not always realize how important they are and that they can be improved! Your teachers and lecturers will help you with tips, techniques and opportunities to practise these skills, but you should also work on them yourself. Make a note of the list and make sure they are built into your study programme.

- reading and comprehending written text
- summarizing text and making notes from text
- listening
- note-taking from videos and lectures
- writing up notes
- using abbreviations
- revision techniques.

If you are going on to do a degree, you will certainly need these skills well honed!

## Record-keeping

Make sure that you keep the following up-to-date for your Portfolio of Evidence

- vocational tracking sheets
- core skills tracking sheets
- assignments and assignment front sheets.

These record sheets will be provided by the unit lecturers on your course.

## Skills you will be developing

- independent learning
- research
- working in teams
- presentation skills of a high standard – both in presenting work and making presentations
- note-taking
- listening, speaking and writing
- extracting and/or summarizing information from texts.

## Note-taking

You will need to learn how to write quickly and take down the important information contained in a lecture or class discussion. Note-taking is a skill which has to be developed and practised. There are techniques in note-taking and you should be given help and advice during your course, and the chance to practise.

One important habit to get into is to write up your notes as soon a possible after making them, and when the information is still fresh i your mind. If you don't do this, unless you are a superb note-take you will probably find you can't make any sense of your notes whe you need to refer to them!

## Know how you learn

There isn't space here to discuss the different methods of learning. Bu I do want to point out, and it is important for you to remember, tha *we don't all learn in the same way*. Your friend or the person next to yo may have one way of learning. If you don't learn in the same way a that person, it doesn't mean their way is necessarily better or that yo are in any way less clever. Know how you learn best and stick to it.

And please, ask questions whenever you don't understand some thing. In any communication, you, as the receiver of the informatio are the most important person. Remember this and never be frightene to ask questions. And I can almost guarantee that when you do ask question you will find that you are not the only person who hasn understood!

### GOOD LUCK WITH YOUR STUDIES!

# 8

# Going on to Higher Education

*'The university said they were impressed with my application. I was delighted because the course and the facilities they offer made it my first choice, and I'm really enjoying being an undergraduate.'*
Shirazul

---

### CHAPTER SUMMARY

This chapter tells you what to consider when applying to a higher education institution (HEI). You can read about the achievements of past GNVQ students in Chapter 9. This chapter covers:

▶ decisions you will need to make
▶ completing your UCAS form
▶ entry requirements
▶ European degrees
▶ GNVQs as a preparation for a degree.

---

## GOING ON TO HIGHER EDUCATION

Being a student at university or college should be a wonderful experience – if you plan and choose wisely. There are a number of factors to consider, not least that this will be your life for the next three or four years and will have a considerable influence on the rest of your life. To make this important next step, you will need to make decisions about the following:

- to live at home or independently
- the course and content
- what size, type, location and facilities of university/college
- entry requirements.

Going on to higher education, more than taking employment, mean
you may have to or want to consider moving away from home. If yo
have the choice, then many would extol the benefits and person
development in 'going away' to university and living in halls of res
dence or sharing accommodation with other students.

There is a wide diversity of courses to choose from: from singl
honours to combined honours to modular and HNDs. This gives yo
the opportunity to identify or tailor a course that best suits you an
fits in with your career aspirations.

Then, of course, what HEI? Where is the university or college sit
ated and what does the surrounding area have to offer? Do you war
to be in a small/large town or city, or in a rural or coastal setting
What facilities, activities and clubs are offered by the HEI and locally?

And what are the entry requirements for the courses you like? Som
institutions still automatically ask for GCSE maths and English, bu
there are examples where these have been negotiated. More HEIs nov
offer maths and communications workshops, in which case they prob
ably won't ask for GCSEs – they will be more concerned with you
course results and your interest and proven ability for the cours
Entry requirements can be diverse, so know what HEIs will expec
and accept. Your school or college may be in a partnership with a
HEI to create a progression pathway into HE. In brief:

- know your career aspirations
- research your HE opportunities thoroughly
- is your school/college in partnership with an HEI?
- choose a course which interests you and which you will enjoy
- select an HEI where you can make the most of your three or fou
  years
- plan your studies to meet the entry requirements.

## Plan A and Plan B

Plan A is undertaken by thoroughly researching the courses and uni
versities you feel are going to suit you best and fit in with your care
aims and interests, and meeting the HEI's entry requirements. I

theory you could end up on any one of the courses you choose – so make sure you choose where you are going to be happy.

Plan B, hopefully, you won't need to put into action. But it is just as well to be prepared. Plan B is your fail-safe: it is what you would want to do if you don't get the offer you want. In the second term of your second year, it is a good idea to start assessing how well you are doing against your targets. Students who don't get final offers for the courses they selected go into 'clearing'. This is looking at the courses which still have vacancies. It can be a frantic exercise and hasty decisions are often made. If you find yourself in clearing and have thought this through beforehand, you can reduce the pressure and avoid making last-minute panic decisions.

## Making the application

Application to higher education is made during the first term of your second year advanced level course. Your application is made through UCAS (Universities and Colleges Admissions Service) and you can list up to six choices of course. Bear in mind:

- that in processing your completed UCAS form it is reduced in size by about one-third. So you must ensure your form is well presented and legible, otherwise it may become unreadable in its new format!
- also, that because so many people are applying to HE, selection may be made on the basis of the application form alone and *without* an interview.

When the HEIs have gone through the applications and made their decisions, offers to students are made. When you receive your offers, you must indicate:1. your first choice (preferred' offer); and 2. your reserve choice (the 'insurance' offer).

In addition to your choice of six courses, your application includes the following major components:

- your grades (and predicted grades) and achievements
- your personal statement
- a confidential reference by a senior teacher or tutor.

## Personal statement

As well as your grades, a very important part of your application is your personal statement. Apart from clearly linking your GNVQ studies to your chosen higher education course (which it is essential that you do), and convincing the selector that you are motivated to do the course, universities like to know about you as a person and that you will enjoy and gain from the wider activities and experiences of university life.

Too many students don't put enough effort into their personal statement, and others don't do themselves justice. So make sure you work on it and get it right. You will receive help and guidance from the centre where you study.

## Confidential reference

Also on your application form, your teacher or tutor is required to write a confidential reference about you. Although this may not be in keeping with an 'open records' policy (which is allowing people to know what is kept on their file), many, if not the majority of, admissions tutors prefer the reference to be confidential to ensure objectivity. So you must understand what is required to be written by your teacher or tutor, and that you must influence your referee in a positive fashion!

# Which course?

Before you decide on the university and the course, your careers officer will have seen you to discuss opportunities and choices, and your centre will have arranged visits to different universities. Hopefully past students who have gone on to HE will come in and talk to you about their experiences. They can also tell you the importance of developing skills which will help you cope at university. Treat your investigation and selection of HE courses as a research project and make sure you can make an informed decision.

# Entry requirements

Universities will specify grades as part of their entry requirements whether they are A levels or GNVQs. They may also specify GCSEs. The entry requirements will vary from university to university, will depend on the course and the type of degree, ie single honours, joint honours, modular or an HND course. Chapter 9 will give you an idea of the entry requirements asked of past GNVQ students.

The entry requirements of many universities are recorded in a data base compiled by UCAS and NCVQ. The latest edition – *GNVQs and higher education – 1996 entry conditions* – published in September 1995 will be held by centres.

For 18 year olds, the HE requirement may be two or three A levels, BTEC National, Advanced GNVQ, or an equivalent qualification. You will usually need to achieve merit or distinction grades for GNVQs, while some universities may also ask for GNVQ additional units or an A or AS level.

Don't be surprised if GCSEs in maths and English are also entry requirements for some degrees. Universities understand GCSEs and use them as reassurance that students have met a certain standard. As GNVQs are a new qualification, not all universities appreciate the standard of maths required across GNVQ units. There are examples where the level and complexity of calculations used in practical applications for Advanced GNVQs, have been pointed out to university admissions staff and the GCSE maths requirement has been dropped or negotiated.

The equivalence of three A levels may be achieved by:

| Two A levels | plus | either | two AS levels |
| | | or | six GNVQ units |
| | | or | TechBac |
| GNVQ Advanced | plus | either | one A level |
| or BTEC National | | or | two AS levels |
| | | or | six additional GNVQ units |
| | | or | TechBac |

but you will need to check acceptability by the university.

If you are planning to go on to study for an HND or degree, do find out what the entry requirements are so that you know what you must aim to achieve and so avoid later disappointment. The demand for university places is increasing, and you may find some universities are pushing up their entry requirements for degrees. You must check entry requirements with your tutor and careers adviser. Having said that, most schools and colleges have established links with higher education and will prepare their students accordingly. These pathways provide a progression route onto a related degree course.

## GNVQs AS PREPARATION FOR A DEGREE

GNVQs are a good preparation for degrees, especially in related subjects. Students from my college who have gone on to do business degrees from a level 3 business course have not only confirmed this and felt no difference between themselves and A level students, but proved it by achieving distinctions in their first year. Universities have found that students from a GNVQ route have a maturity that A level students don't have, and that GNVQ students are also more able to undertake independent study and research than A level students. GNVQs will also have prepared you well for meeting deadlines, working with others, making presentations, writing reports and using IT.

# EUROPEAN DEGREES

It is not only language degrees which give students the chance to study abroad. Many universities in the UK have now teamed up with universities in Europe. Business students, for example, can take a BA Hons in European Business Studies. These degrees give you the opportunity to study for one or two years in another European country. You can progress to these degrees from an Advanced GNVQ. The majority of these degrees will, of course, need an A level, or post GCSE or equivalent, or otherwise proven fluency in a European language (eg French, German or Spanish) as part of the entry requirements. Some courses will also include the study of additional European languages.

# NOT MADE THE GRADE?

During the course you will be given an opportunity to re-do work or resit external tests, but if your final results should fall short of the entry requirements for the degree you want, you can try for another university, consider a modular degree, or go onto an HND (higher national diploma) course. An HND is usually a two-year course and will take you onto a related degree – usually into the second year of that degree.

**9**

# GNVQ Achievements

*'At 16 I was written off academically, but after GNVQ I am at university and am told I have a very promising career ahead of me.'*
John

---

**CHAPTER SUMMARY**

This part of the book is the 'where are they now?' section. Students on GNVQs have now gone on to higher education and employment, and in this chapter are the destinations of some of those students, many told by themselves, in their own words. Some students only needed to pass their GNVQ, while others took additional units and A and AS levels.

Note: HE stands for Higher Education.

---

## BUSINESS STUDENTS

This is the story of Frances who, with two GCSEs (neither in maths nor English) was able to choose either university or employment when she completed a GNVQ Advanced course.

## FRANCES

I had only achieved two GCSEs at grade C, and I didn't get maths or English. I was quite a shy person but I did want to work in business, or banking or retail management. I stayed on at school and did the Intermediate GNVQ in Business. I really enjoyed this course and gained a Distinction, so I went on to do the Advanced level where I also gained a Distinction. The GNVQs really suited my style of learning and working, and I added five additional units to enhance my studies. I now feel a strong sense of achievement, and I am much more confident and outgoing.

I made HE and job applications. I received a number of offers from universities but the university course of my first choice originally turned me down because I didn't have GCSE maths. They reversed this when the school explained the level and amount of maths involved on the GNVQ Advanced course. I have instead taken a job with a major bank entering at the same grade as an A level student. Although the bank too, needed to be reassured about the level of maths on my course.

## PROTIVA

I wanted a career in accountancy. I achieved five GCSEs, including maths and English, at grade C. However, my results were not good enough to get me on to an A level programme, so I went on to GNVQ Advanced in Business. I took five additional GNVQ units and completed the course with a merit. By taking this route I am now working towards a career in accountancy and studying for an accountancy degree at Liverpool University.

# ART & DESIGN STUDENTS

This is John's story. He left school with grades D and E for the nine GCSEs he sat. On his GNVQ, he obtained national recognition as a 'young engineer'.

## JOHN

I lacked self-confidence after GCSEs. I hadn't achieved anything. So I went to college and enrolled on a C&G Diploma in Vocational Education (a Foundation level course) with an engineering option. The college was piloting GNVQs and I continued my studies through to

Advanced GNVQ in Art & Design. I also chose to take an A level in Design and Technology.

As part of the coursework, I designed and built a recumbent bike and I was selected to represent North Yorkshire engineers at the CBI Conference celebrating 'Manufacturing by Design' at the International Conference Centre in Birmingham in 1994. My work was put on exhibition at the Conference. I am now at Coventry university studying Industrial Design. I only needed to pass the Advanced GNVQ. The university said they liked my portfolio of work.

At 16 I was written off academically, but after GNVQ I am at university and am told I have a very promising career ahead of me.

This is the story of Derek, a student who had to revise his progression in the light of his results.

## DEREK

I left school in 1992 with one GCSE in Art & Design, but I knew I wanted to be a graphic designer. I discussed my ambition with staff and careers advisers at school and decided to take the Intermediate GNVQ in Art & Design at college. I expected to be working mostly on computers and high-tech equipment. We did that, but we also did a lot of other things – such as fine art, still life and textiles. I wasn't sure at first, but I'm glad now because it opened my eyes to a wider view of art. I went on to the Advanced level and became interested in typography and desk-top publishing. At first there seemed to be a lot of repetition, but the course gave me the opportunity to specialize. During my first year I resat GCSE English, but was again unsuccessful.

I wanted to carry on with my studies so I made applications to do a BA degree in graphics. I was invited for interview by St Martins College in London. I thought the interview went ok. They were pleasantly interested in my portfolio and seemed to know what a GNVQ was. But I didn't get an offer. I had also applied to the London College of Printing, but I didn't even get an interview. So I decided to examine other routes into higher education. I am now studying for an HND in Art & Design which with further study I can convert to a degree. The HND is more academic than the GNVQ. It also shows very clearly what is done in industry. I think I'm really going to enjoy it. I am also making another attempt at GCSE English. Let's hope its third time lucky! I am very glad I did GNVQs. They are great for introducing you to a broad range of skills in art. There is plenty of practical work and a chance to try out new techniques.

### WILL

I finished school with very good GCSEs. I wanted to study Art although the only art I had done previously was in middle school. I did an Art GCSE in one year and was encouraged when I achieved a B grade. I then took A level Art and gained an A grade. I then decided to do the Advanced GNVQ in Art & Design, and I have obtained a place at Sheffield Hallam to follow their popular Product Design and Packaging degree. The university made me an unconditional offer on completion of the GNVQ. I was pleased when they said they had been impressed with my GNVQ portfolio.

# LEISURE & TOURISM STUDENTS

Caroline, whose aim is to work for an airline when she can apply at the age of 21, tells her story.

### CAROLINE

My ambition is to work for an airline, as a member of the cabin crew, when I am 21. After I left school, with nine GCSEs including English, maths and French, I went on to the Advanced GNVQ in Leisure & Tourism to learn about the industry and to gain a qualification. The course has helped me a lot. It was very interesting and it gave me the opportunity to cover a wide area of study – which included customer service and customer care, and hospitality and catering. I worked at an airline check-in at Gatwick for my work placement. This was very useful experience and I was also able to observe the wider practices and procedures carried out by an airline. I added to my studies a language unit on French for business which is more directly related to using the language in the work situation than GCSE. I believe it helps to have another language.

I started work when I completed the GNVQ. I began as a receptionist for a major British holiday group in their newest and key hotel in London. After eight months I was promoted to Head Receptionist and am now responsible for the front-of-house staff. A particular benefit from the course was learning how to work with people and how to work in teams, as well as dealing with customers and clients. I am very glad I did the GNVQ and I know employers are looking for these skills.

This is the story of Jessica who loves travel, and was advised to obtain qualifications to help her reach her career ambition.

## JESSICA

I have a real love of travel, and I wanted to travel abroad and work as an air hostess or a courier when I left school. I had three GCSEs at B grade. They told me at school that I should get some more qualifications and so I tried the Advanced GNVQ in Leisure & Tourism. It was a great course and I really loved it. I had not been expecting to study aspects of the leisure industry, but I found them enjoyable. The business aspects were also new experiences and were quite difficult but they opened my eyes to the range of skills needed to be successful in tourism. And I did have to resit some of the external tests. I made the decision to start university after college. During the course, my trips abroad satisfied my desire to travel. I knew that if I took a year out I probably wouldn't want to come back.

I made a number of applications to do a BA degree in Travel and Tourism and received several offers. My favourite was from Luton University who wanted 18 units with an overall Merit. At that time I was working towards 17 units, but as my college was running a Summer School I signed on to take an extra unit. I am now at Luton, and the modular structure of the course allows plenty of freedom and choice. I am certainly pleased with the pathway I have taken to reach my aim of working and travelling abroad. My advice to anyone doing a GNVQ would be to keep up with the assignments. Missing deadlines can be bad for your health!

## JOHN

I was not considered academic and I felt frustrated that I wasn't achieving. That is until I started on the Advanced Leisure & Tourism course. I partly chose this course because I am keen on sport, and in particular I am very good at karate and have a keen interest in Japan.

The Advanced Leisure & Tourism course opened up new vistas and opportunities for me. I didn't complete the whole course because I suddenly saw how I could pursue my interest in Japan and visit that country. I had to raise funds to finance my stay in Japan – which I begin towards the end of 1995. I do, however, leave the course with credits for the work I have done, and it is always open to me to complete the units for the full qualification. I am much happier about my achievements and feel I now have some control over my life and can give it direction.

# HEALTH & SOCIAL CARE STUDENTS

Jackie is a student who very nearly dropped out from school but found the right stimulation from GNVQ courses.

## JACKIE

I didn't like school, and I very nearly didn't finish. But I decided to go on to college, because I knew I wanted to be a primary school teacher. I enrolled on the Intermediate GNVQ in Health & Social Care. At last I found a course which I really enjoyed and I gained a Merit. I went on to do an Advanced GNVQ. I really found the teaching and learning styles on a GNVQ suited me, and I could focus on something I was good at. I liked the level of responsibility we were given and the range of practical work we undertook. I have gained a lot of skills and knowledge and developed personally.

I have now been accepted to do a teacher training degree on the strength of my portfolio and my UCAS statement.

This is about Nick whose ambition is to work in the medical profession. The scope of a GNVQ has helped him to manage change in realising his ambition.

## NICK

I left school in 1991 with five GCSEs at grade C and above. I knew I wanted to work within the medical profession in some capacity so I went to college to take a one-year pre-nursing programme. During that year I became aware of some of the options available to me. I became interested in working as a paramedic or an operating department assistant so I decided to take the Advanced GNVQ in Health & Social Care. I quickly became accustomed to the course and enjoyed the new approach to study and assessment. I also began an AS in psychology, which I found challenging. The essays were hard but the AS mode of study was such a contrast to GNVQ that I decided to drop psychology and take additional GNVQ units instead.

During the second year, we had a visit from the army and I decided that I wanted to work as a combat medical technician. The work seemed very interesting and the fitness side interested me as well. The army recognized the Advanced GNVQ as an entry qualification. I applied and was accepted, and I looked forward to progression and promotion. Unfortunately, I received leg injuries and was discharged from the army on medical grounds. I was then out of work, and this was a bad time for me. I visited the job centre regularly and found work after about 12 weeks. I am now working as a part-time care assistant in a residential nursing home for the elderly. It's a lot better than I expected and I really find the work rewarding. I hope to become full-time as soon as possible. However, my aim is still to work as a paramedic or operating medical assistant. I would certainly recommend GNVQs. I think they can open up lots of opportunities, and in unexpected areas.'

## NEIL

When I was 23, I decided to return to study. I had left school without any qualifications despite being told I was a bright student. At college I enrolled on a fast track Intermediate/Advanced GNVQ programme to test my study skills. Being successful on the five-month Intermediate programme led me on to the roll-on Advanced course, and I achieved a Distinction. I am now studying for a degree in psychology.

## RUTH

I had a poor profile at GCSEs and felt a failure, but I was advised to try the Pre-Advanced Health course at my local college. This course gives students the opportunity to resit GCSE exams and also to study appropriate science and health based topics. On this course, I achieved 4 GCSEs grades A–C (excluding maths) and progressed to the Advanced GNVQ in Health & Social Care. In the first year, I resat maths GCSE and gained a C grade. For the GNVQ I achieved a merit grade. I wanted to go on to HE and I received two offers to study Podiatry at university and I chose Edinburgh. GNVQs have allowed me to develop much more than my academic profile. I feel much more confident in all situations, including being able to give good oral reports and manage my time effectively.

## NICOLA

I left school with a poor academic record and went out to work. I wasn't doing as well as I wanted so I decided to return to study to improve my career opportunities. The Advanced GNVQ Health & Social Care suited me perfectly, and I am now studying for a BA in occupational therapy.

# MANUFACTURING STUDENTS

In a recently published Casebook, *Manufacturing GNVQ. Working for you,* published by NCVQ, Advanced GNVQ Manufacturing students at Huddersfield New College in Yorkshire were interviewed. The students' view of the course is that it has improved their employment opportunities as they have experienced first-hand the benefits and excitement of working in modern manufacturing. This is what they have said about the course:

'The manufacturing course is an excellent alternative to A level. It covers a wide variety of skills and topics, is work-related, and provides good links with industries in the community.'

Matthew, second year student

'This course gives you a much better chance of getting into a career in a manufacturing industry of your choice . . . Manufacturing GNVQ also teaches you about technology, information technology, communication and mathematics, all in the same course.'

Shaheez, first year student

'It enables you to go into an expanding industry where you can affect the quality of your everyday life.'

Graham, second year student

Matthew and Graham were sponsored by Zeneca (a pharmaceuticals and agrochemicals company) and are now training with Zeneca to be an engineering technician and a chemical process technician. As well as the GNVQ, but not required for employment with Zeneca, Matthew took an additional GNVQ unit in electrical principles for manufacturing, and an AS level Chemistry. Graham was already studying A level Physics when he began his GNVQ course and added AS Chemistry. Zeneca's sponsorship included lectures by its staff, visits to the plant and paid work experience.

# A FEW PEN PORTRAITS OF GNVQ STUDENTS

- A student who wanted to study for a BEd, so that she could teach and specialize in maths at a primary school, was denied a place at university because she did not have A level maths. She negotiated a place at a university by being able to offer numeracy skills at Level 4.

- A student with six GCSEs (which included a retake of English) followed Advanced GNVQ in Business. He chose a language unit in German as one of the optional units and enhanced his GNVQ with three additional units. He was asked for an overall merit to go on and study for a European business degree.
- A business student is now employed by Travis Perkins and sponsored by the company to do an HND. He was one of two appointed from 300 applicants. He found that the financial work he did on his GNVQ has been extremely useful in his HND work.
- A student achieving a distinction at Advanced level Art & Design, enhancing her studies with a vocational certificate in Aerobics, has gone on to HE to study for a BA in sports studies and art.
- A student with a distinction in Advanced Art & Design, who took a further year to achieve additional units from Advanced Health & Social Care to prepare her for study, is now on a BA degree in applied art and design.
- Two students who followed the Advanced Leisure & Tourism course at John Ruskin College, Croydon, and were involved in the business enterprise based on Hever Station, were headhunted for employment by EuroStar and Network SouthCentral.
- A business student was asked for a distinction plus a grade C for the sociology A level he was studying for a degree in American studies.
- A business student who had travelled independently in Egypt and Israel and whose ambition is to become a senior executive of a large multinational company, was asked for either a distinction and three additional units, or a distinction for 12 units and a C grade for the A level he was studying to do a business degree.
- A student had three GCSEs including maths and English. He was not thought of as an academic student and after GCSEs he followed a vocational path. He did the C&G Diploma in Vocational Education moving up to Advanced GNVQ where he achieved a distinction. He enhanced his GNVQ with four additional units. This student also had to work part-time to help support his family. He received several offers to study for a degree in Business.
- A student now studying for a business and law degree achieved the entry requirement of GNVQ at merit plus six points, ie A level at grade C or above.
- A student with distinctions at Intermediate and Advanced levels, and an A level in English language and literature, is now studying a BA degree in business studies.

# Glossary

**Additional studies**  Any studies that you may decide to do alongside your GNVQ that are not required for the full GNVQ award. For example, they may be GNVQ additional units, GCSEs, A or AS levels, or TechBac qualifications.

**Additional units**  Accredited GNVQ units studied with and over and above the requirements for a full qualification, or studied independently. These units can be added to enhance or widen your studies.

**APL**  Accreditation of prior learning. This is recognition, or being accredited for already having achieved the level of competence required for parts of the syllabus. You must show evidence of your competence to allow this to be counted towards the qualification.

**Assessment**  Assessment is continuous on a GNVQ programme, and is made on coursework. It is carried out by the teachers (assessors) and an internal verifier at your centre, and validated by an external verifier appointed by the awarding body. (*See* Vocational awarding body.)

**Assessors and verifiers**  'Assessors' are the teachers on a GNVQ course who carry out the assessment of students' work. Their assessment is checked to ensure GNVQ standards are met by another member of staff who is the 'internal verifier'. Students' work, and the standard maintained by the centre, are further checked by an outside person appointed by the awarding body. This person is known as the 'external verifier'. (*See also* Verifiers.)

**BTEC**  Business & Technology Education Council – an examinations board and a GNVQ awarding body.

**C&G**  City & Guilds of London Institute, commonly referred to as City & Guilds – an examinations board and a GNVQ awarding body.

**Core skills**  The skills associated with being able to communicate, work with numbers, and use information technology in both a personal and professional capacity. These core skills are mandatory and integrated in each course of study. Additional core skills units are available in personal skills and problem-solving skills. Core skills can be achieved up to Level 5.

**Credit accumulation**  Each unit achieved is certificated, and the student receives a credit for that unit. The accumulation of credits in a vocational area leads to the full award of the GNVQ. There is no time limit attached to completing the credits for a full GNVQ.

**Element**  An area or topic of study within a unit. Each Element will specify Performance criteria, Range, and Evidence indicators. There will be between two and five Elements in each unit.

**Evidence indicators**  An explanation of the work to be produced to pass an Element.

**External tests**  These are unit tests set by the awarding bodies. Questions cover the whole of the curriculum for the unit. They are usually one hour long, and made up of 25–40 multiple-choice questions. A 70% pass mark is usually required. These tests are under review and may become more varied.

**GNVQs**  General National Vocational Qualifications – vocational alternatives to GCSEs and GCE A levels.

**Grade/grading/interim grading**  The grade is the overall level of achievement on completion of a full GNVQ. One of three grades will be awarded: pass, merit or distinction. The overall grade is determined by the standard of coursework against grading criteria which are based on four 'themes'. To achieve a merit or distinction grade, 30% or more of the coursework must fulfil that standard of the grading criteria. During the course, you will receive 'interim grading indications' on the work you do.

**Grading criteria**  All work is assessed against the four performance areas or 'themes' which make up the grading criteria: the ability to plan; to seek and handle information; to evaluate; and the quality of the work.

**GSVQs**  General Scottish Vocational Qualifications – the Scottish equivalent to GNVQs.

**HE/HEIs**  Higher Education and Higher Education Institutions

**Induction**  At the start of the GNVQ, an introductory programme to explain the structure, content and organization of the course.

**Integration**  This is relating areas of study so that learning is not in isolation. Core skills are integrated with the syllabus to demonstrate the use of skills in practice; and coursework may span more than one unit to integrate studies and bring together learning to undertake a task or project.

**Languages Lead Body**  The body responsible for setting the standard of language units.

**Level**  Identifies the level of study. There are three levels of GNVQ: Level 1 is Foundation; Level 2 is Intermediate; Level 3 is Advanced. Core skills can be achieved up to Level 5.

## All you need to know about GNVQs

**Mandatory units**   The compulsory units which form the basis of the curriculum at each level for every vocational area. Includes vocational and core skills units.

**Modular programme**   A GNVQ programme is modular because it is made up of units (modules), each free-standing and certificated. Completion of the required number of units (depending on the level) within a vocational area leads to a full award.

**National framework of qualifications**   Academic and vocational qualifications of equal status offering alternative pathways of study.

**NCVQ**   National Council for Vocational Qualifications – the body with overall responsibility for GNVQs and NVQs.

**NRA**   National Record of Achievement. This records ambitions, qualifications, achievements, testimonials and references. It has been introduced nationwide in schools and continued through college into university and beyond. As a portfolio of an individual's abilities and interests, it is of interest to education and employers.

**NVQs**   National Vocational Qualifications. Based on tasks performed in the workplace, so the opportunity for people in work to obtain qualifications.

**Optional units**   The units of choice taken in addition to the mandatory units and which make up the full GNVQ qualification.

**Part One GNVQ**   A vocational option for 14 year olds as part of the National Curriculum. Six units (three vocational, three core skills) at GNVQ Foundation or Intermediate level in Business, Health & Social Care, and Manufacturing. Currently being piloted, but from 1997 should be available to all school students at age 14. Part One is a qualification in its own right, and accepted as credit towards a full GNVQ.

**Pathway**   May refer to three things. In education, the academic and/or vocational route taken to achieve qualifications. In GNVQs, a vocational pathway is the selection of optional units which lead to specialization within a vocational area. Pathway (or partnership) may also be the term used by centres for their established links with HEIs which assist progression into HE for students.

**Performance criteria**   Describe the depth of study for an Element. The Performance criteria list what the student must be able to carry out.

**Portfolio of evidence**   The collection of coursework and test results which is evidence that course requirements and grading criteria have been met. The final award of a GNVQ depends on the production of the portfolio as it is part of the final evaluation.

**Range**   The Range identifies aspects of the industry or service (covered by the vocational area) to be taken into account. It broadens study by relating and applying the Performance Criteria to the operation and workings of the industry or service as a whole. A Range is given for each Element.

**RSA**   Royal Society of Arts – an examinations board and a GNVQ awarding body.

**UCAS**   Universities and Colleges Admissions Service – the body receiving and processing applications for higher education courses.

**Unit**   A defined area of study for a GNVQ programme. There are mandatory, optional, core skills and additional units. Mandatory, optional and core skills units are combined to make up the study within a vocational area for a full GNVQ; additional units are added to enhance the qualification. Each unit is certificated with the exception of the Problem-Solving core skills units.

**Verifiers**   The 'internal verifier' is a member of staff at a centre who checks the assessment of students' work to ensure GNVQ standards have been met. An 'external verifier' is an outside person appointed by the awarding body who ensures a centre is applying the appropriate standards in assessing students' work. The external verifier will also advise on improving quality.

**Vocational awarding bodies**   The examinations boards which have been authorized to offer GNVQs: currently BTEC, C&G and RSA.

# Helpful Publications

The following are only some of the publications available that will be or could be of interest or help to you. The list is therefore not definitive, but I hope it will indicate the range of materials published to help you on your way!

## GNVQs – GENERAL

NCVQ and the three awarding bodies publish GNVQ material for students. Approach them direct for a publications list.

*GNVQ Scholarship Scheme – a guide*
issued by NCVQ

### Kogan Page titles

*How to Pass A levels and GNVQs*
Howard Barlow
£5.99 ISBN: 0 7494 1556 8

*Getting to Grips with GNVQs*
Geoff Hayward
£16.95 ISBN: 0 7494 1421 9
*British Vocational Qualifications*
annual directory of vocational qualifications available from all awarding bodies in Britain
£30

# FOR GNVQ BUSINESS STUDENTS

The following Longman books take students through the language and processes of a GNVQ, for example, how to collect evidence.

*Introduction to Business GNVQ: Foundation*
J Boyce
£4.99 ISBN: 0582 274168

*Introduction to Business GNVQ: Intermediate*
J Boyce
£4.99 ISBN: 0582 274176

*Introduction to Business GNVQ: Advanced*
M Buckley
£4.99 ISBN: 0582 246105

# FOR GNVQ HEALTH & SOCIAL CARE STUDENTS

The following Longman books take students through the language and processes of a GNVQ, for example, how to collect evidence.

*Introduction to GNVQ: Foundation*
Pip Hardy
£4.99 ISBN: 0582 255139

*Introduction to GNVQ: Intermediate*
Pip Hardy
£4.99 ISBN: 0582 255147

*Introduction to GNVQ: Advanced*
Pip Hardy
£4.99 ISBN: 0582 255155

# FOR GNVQ MANUFACTURING STUDENTS

*Manufacturing GNVQ. Working for You*
(Case studies of people employed in various fields of manufacturing. Each case study indicates how Intermediate and Advanced GNVQ Manufacturing courses would give a headstart in the employee's job.)
Available free from the Publications Department of NCVQ.

# CORE SKILLS

*Core Skills: Students Book*
Cathy Lake, project manager
published by Longman
£2.50 ISBN: 0582 249724
(This book tells students how to identify, use and record core skills.)

# LEARNING/STUDY SKILLS

*The Learning Skills series*
Published by Collins Education and the National Extension College
(NEC), this series includes the following titles, each priced at £8.35:

*How to use your dictionary*
*How to study effectively*
*How to succeed in exams and assessments*
*Clear thinking*
*How to manage your study time*
*How to improve your memory*
*How to write reports*

*Study Skills for GCSE and A Level*
Michael Montgomery
published by Letts Educational 1991
£4.95 ISBN: 1–85758–017–6

# LOOKING AHEAD

*What's next for me? Planning your first steps after school*
Hertfordshire County Careers and CRAC
published by Hobsons
£5.99 ISBN:1–85324–512–7

*GNVQs and higher education – 1996 entry conditions*
A database compiled by UCAS and NCVQ
Published September 1995.
A copy is sent to all GNVQ centres.

*UCAS University and College Entrance Official Guide 1996*
(A list of HEIs, courses and entry requirements)
Published in association with *The Independent* and Letts Study Guides
£12

*How to Complete your UCAS Form for 1996 entry to University & College*
Tony Higgins
published by Trotman 1995
£5.95 ISBN: 0–85660–183–7
(Tony Higgins is the Chief Executive of UCAS.)

*Sponsorship for Students – an essential guide to sponsorship*
(For all students seeking sponsorship for degrees/HND courses.)
CRAC
published by Hobsons
£7.95 cover price but available at £5.95 ISBN:1–86017–135–4

*What do graduates do? 1995*
(Careers information for those going on to HE.)
AgCAS (Association of Graduate Careers Advisory Services) and
CRAC
published by Hobsons
£5.95 ISBN: 1–85324–958–0

*Building your career: Sixth Form choices 1996*
(Case studies with information on employers/jobs and HEIs/courses,
told by employees and students. Includes articles on moving on to HE
and choosing a course, a guide to grants and loans, taking a year out,
career options, finding a job, and 'diary dates' for applying to HE.)
published by Hobsons
£8.50

# STUDENTS' YEAR OUT OPPORTUNITIES

If you are considering taking a 'year out' before or after university, the
following are some of the organizations which can help you. If your
'gap year' is before university, don't forget to apply to the university
for a 'deferred entry'.

Central Bureau for Visits and Exchanges
Seymour Mews House
Seymour Mews,
London W1H 9PE
tel: 0171 486 5101

GAP Activity Project
44 Queens Road
Reading RG1 4BB
tel: 01734 594 914

Project Trust
Breacachadh Castle
Isle of Coll
Argyle PA78 6TB
tel: 01879 230 444

VSO
317 Putney Bridge Road
London SW15 2AN
tel: 0181 780 2266

# JOBHUNTING

*The Jobseeker's Guide to Success*
Sue O'Rourke
published by The Pentland Press 1995
£7.50 ISBN:1–85821–335–5

# IN HE AND BEYOND

AgCAS is the professional association of careers service in higher education, including all universities and most of the major colleges within HE throughout the British Isles.

AgCAS publishes a range of materials, both general and job specific (including working for an EU institution or working in a continental European country). Publications and videos, mainly aimed at undergraduates and graduates (including mature students) seeking employment, can be found in the Careers Service in HEIs.

For a catalogue of publications contact:

Richard Hill
AgCAS Administration Manager
Careers Advisory Service
University of Sheffield
8–10 Favell Road
Sheffield S3 7QX
tel: 0114 2753381

AgCAS videos (entertaining as well as informative), each priced inclusive of VAT £50 (£30 to education) include:

*Why am I here?*
How to acquire transferable skills at university, and the skills employers look for.

*Starting Points*
– about career choice, and how the best decisions are made as a result of having information: about yourself, jobs and employers.

And three videos which cover the whole job application process:

*Write giving full details*
– how to fill in job applications. Aimed at final year undergraduates.

*Tell me, Mr Dunstone*
– how to get through your first interview. Aimed at final year undergraduates.

*Two Whole Days*
– about the 'two-day assessment' selection procedure now increasingly used by employers.

CRAC and Hobsons Casebooks provide case studies on graduate employment and professional courses. Held by university libraries and careers offices. Each casebook includes case studies by graduates on the work they do, qualifications on entry and any further studies. They are published by Hobsons, each priced £8.50, and cover the following areas:

Science/Physics
Engineering
Marketing, retailing & sales
Law
IT
Finance
Public Sector
City
MBA
Mature Students
Equal Opportunities: Working Women and their careers
Disability

**All you need to know about GNVQs**

CRAC (Careers Research and Advisory Centre) is an independent education and development agency which specialises in setting up courses, conferences, management skills and training programmes, evaluation reports and innovative development work to aid career choice and life-long learning. It is not part of the careers service and does not offer individual career advice. CRAC publications are available through

Hobsons Publishing plc
Bateman Street
Cambridge CB2 1LZ
tel: 01223 354551
CRAC can be contacted on 01223 460277.

# Useful Addresses

**BTEC**
Business Technology &
   Education Council
Central House
Upper Woburn Place
London WC1H 0HH
Tel: 0171 413 8400

**C&G**
City & Guilds of London
   Institute
1 Giltspur Street
London EC1A 9DD
Tel: 0171 294 2468

**Languages Lead Body**
c/o CILT
20 Bedfordbury
London WC2N 4LB
Tel: 0171 379 5134

**NCVQ**
National Council for Vocational
   Qualifications
222 Euston Road
London NW1 2BZ
Tel: 0171 387 9898

**RSA Examinations Board**
Westwood Way
Coventry CV4 8HS
Tel: 01203 470033

**SCOTVEC**
Scottish Vocational Education
   Council
Hanover House
24 Douglas Street
Glasgow G2 7NQ
General Enquiries
   tel: 0141 248 7900
Publications unit
   tel: 0141 242 2168

**UCAS**
Universities and Colleges
   Admissions Service
Fulton House
Jessop Avenue
Cheltenham
Gloucester GL50 3SH
Tel: 0242 227788 (for guidance
   on admissions procedures only)

# Index